NATIONAL GEOGRAPHIC
Reach™
Language • Literacy • Content

 NATIONAL GEOGRAPHIC LEARNING |  CENGAGE Learning®

Contents

Unit 1: My Family

Unit 2: Shoot for the Sun

Unit 3: To Your Front Door

Unit 4: Growing and Changing

Unit 5: Creature Features

Unit 6: Up In the Air

Unit 7: Then and Now

Unit 8: Get Out the Map!

Unit Concept Map

My Family

Make a concept map with the answers to the Big Question:
What makes a family?

What makes a family?

Name ________________________ Date ____________

Thinking Map: Idea Web

Organize Ideas

Write about what your family does together.

eats meals

watchEz
Tv

What My Family Does Together

GoEz
Outside

Name _____   Date _____

Family Fun

Grammar Rules Nouns

1. A noun names a person.

   My <u>sister</u> and I play together.

2. A noun names a place.

   Eunji plays in the <u>park</u>.

3. A noun names a thing.

   My family lives in a <u>house</u>.

Draw a line under each noun. Then write *person, place,* **or** *thing.*

1. First we eat a big <u>breakfast</u>.

2. Then we go to the park.

3. My father runs with me.

4. My friend meets us there.

5. We play with a ball.

6. Finally we go home.

thing

 Take turns with a partner. Say clues for a person, place, or thing in the room. Have your partner guess the noun.

1.3

Name _____   Date _____

Families in Many Cultures

1 Families live around the world.

2 Families do many things together.
They help each other.
They eat together.

3 Families celebrate.
They play together.
They laugh together.

National Geographic Learning, a part of Cengage Learning, Inc.

Grammar: Singular and Plural Nouns

One or More

Grammar Rules Singular and Plural Nouns

1. A singular noun names one person, place, or thing.

   I have one <u>sister.</u>

2. A plural noun names more than one. Add *s* to most nouns to show more than one.

   You have two <u>sisters.</u>

Write the singular or plural noun.

1. one meal

two _meals_

2. one _____

three brothers

3. one holiday

four _____

4. one _____

two mothers

5. one park

three _____

6. one _____

four sons

💬 **Take turns with a partner. Say and spell the plural nouns.**

Name _____   Date _____

Yes or No?

1. Listen to the questions. Write the Key Word where it belongs in each sentence.
2. Listen to the questions again.
3. Check yes or no for each question.

	Yes	No

1. Is breakfast a _____ _meal_ _____ ? ☑ ☐

2. Is a teacher a _____ ? ☐ ☐

3. Can an apartment be a _____ ? ☐ ☐

4. Is New Year's Day a _____ ? ☐ ☐

5. Can you _____ a birthday? ☐ ☐

6. Is a group of students a _____? ☐ ☐

Families in Many Cultures

Write what the families do together in the Idea Web.

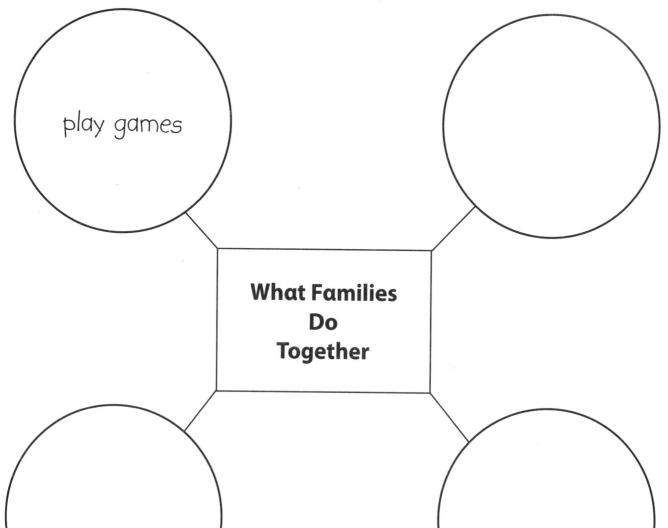

 Take turns with a partner. Tell what you learned about families in "Families in Many Cultures."

National Geographic Learning, a part of Cengage Learning, Inc.

Fluency: Phrasing

Families in Many Cultures

Use this passage to practice reading with proper phrasing.

Families celebrate holidays.   3

Families celebrate birthdays.   6

Phrasing

B ☐ Rarely pauses while reading the text.   A ☐ Frequently pauses at appropriate points in the text.

I ☐ Occasionally pauses while reading the text.   AH ☐ Consistently pauses at appropriate points in the text.

Accuracy and Rate Formula

Use the formula to measure a reader's accuracy and rate while reading aloud.

_____ − _____ = _____

words attempted   number of errors   words correct per
in one minute   minute (wcpm)

Name _____   Date _____

Compare Author's Purpose

Compare "Families in Many Cultures" and "The World Is Your Family".

"Families in Many Cultures"	"The World Is Your Family"
to show families in different places	

 Take turns with a partner. Tell how the authors' purposes are different.

Grammar: Plural Nouns

Name It!

Grammar Rules Plural Nouns

- Add *s* to most nouns to show more than one.

  meal → meal<u>s</u>

- Add *es* to nouns that end with *ss, x, ch,* and *sh* to show more than one.

  lunch → lunch<u>es</u>

glass	sandwich	teacher	mother
meal			lunch
BEGIN			park
			box
END			
brother	dish	class	bowl

1. Play with a partner.
2. Use a small object for a game piece.
3. Flip a coin.

   = Move 1 space.

   = Move 2 spaces.

4. Say the singular noun.
5. Write the plural form on another sheet of paper.
6. The first one to the **END** wins!

Name _____   Date _____

Identify Setting

Write the setting of a family story you know at the top of the left column. Write about the setting below. Draw a picture of the setting in the right column.

Setting: _____	Picture of the Place
•	
•	
•	

Name _____   Date _____

Common or Proper?

Grammar Rules Common and Proper Nouns

1. A common noun names any person, place, or thing.
These nouns do not start with a capital letter.

The girl goes to school.

2. A proper noun names a specific person, place, or thing.
These nouns start with a capital letter.

Maria goes to Franklin Elementary School.

Circle the proper noun in each sentence. Underline the common nouns.

1. (Nan) is my sister.

2. We live in a state called Texas.

3. Max is my dog.

4. My father lives in Dallas.

5. My sister and I always have fun with Papá.

6. We go to Elm Park to play ball.

 Write a sentence about where you live. Have a partner read it aloud and circle the proper noun.

Papá and Me

1 The boy and his papá have many ideas for the day. They walk. They hold hands.

2 They go to the park. They draw pictures. They ride the bus.

3 The boy and his papá hug the boy's grandparents.

Grammar: Proper Nouns

Meet My Family

Grammar Rules Proper Nouns

1. A proper noun names a specific person, place, animal, or thing.
2. Always start a proper noun with a capital letter.

Mario lives in Arizona with his dog, Buster.

Read each sentence. Circle the word or words that need a capital letter. Write the word or words.

1. This is my sister (carla). .... Carla

2. This is my uncle juan. --------------------

3. He lives in houston. -----------------------

4. My aunt rosa lives there, too. ------------

5. Her dog's name is spot. -------------------

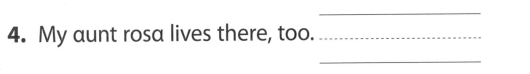

Write a sentence about a family member. Have a partner read it aloud and circle the proper noun.

Vocabulary: Apply Word Knowledge

Family Trip Bingo

1. Write one Key Word in each suitcase.

2. Listen to the clues. Place a marker on the Key Word.

3. Say "Bingo" when you have four markers in a row.

Reread and Summarize: Setting Chart

Papá and Me

List the places that Papá and his son went. Then list words that tell what the places are like.

Places	What the Places are Like
• home	• fun
•	•
•	•
•	•

Take turns with a partner. Use your Setting Chart to give information about the story.

Fluency: Intonation

Papá and Me

Use this passage to practice reading with proper intonation.

We share stories on the bus.   6

Our stop, our stop!   10

Intonation

B ☐ Does not change pitch.   A ☐ Changes pitch to match some of the content.

I ☐ Changes pitch, but does not match content.   AH ☐ Changes pitch to match all of the content.

Accuracy and Rate Formula

Use the formula to measure a reader's accuracy and rate while reading aloud.

_____ - _____ = _____
words attempted   number of errors   words correct per
in one minute   minute (wcpm)

Respond and Extend: T Chart

Compare Genres

Compare a story and a postcard.

Realistic Fiction	Postcard
is a made up story that seems real	is a message from a real person

💬 Tell a partner how a story and a postcard are different.

National Geographic Learning, a part of Cengage Learning, Inc.

Grammar: Proper Nouns

Name Game

Grammar Rules Proper Nouns

Start a proper noun with a capital letter.

My dog Mac is the best dog in the world.

1. **Play with a partner.**

2. **Spin the spinner.**

3. **Name a proper noun. Write the proper noun on a piece of paper.**

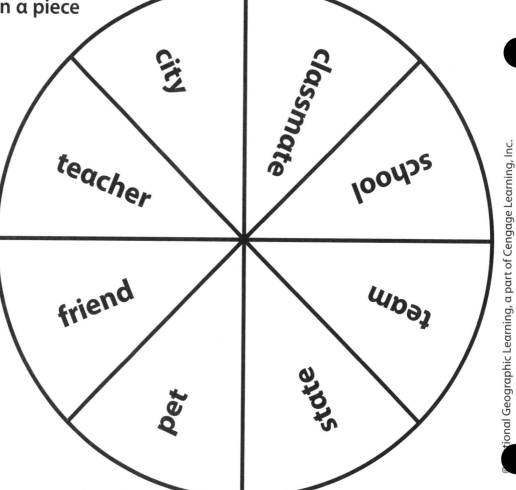

Make a Spinner

1. Put a paper clip ⎯⎯ in the center of the circle.

2. Hold one end of the paper clip with a pencil.

3. Spin the paper clip around the pencil.

Name _____   Date _____

Organization

	Is the writing well-organized? Does it fit the writer's purpose?	Does the writing flow?
4	❏ The writing is very well-organized. ❏ It clearly fits the writer's purpose.	❏ The writing is smooth and logical. Each sentence flows into the next one.
3	❏ Most of the writing is organized. ❏ It mostly fits the writer's purpose.	❏ Most of the writing is smooth. There are only a few sentences that do not flow logically.
2	❏ The writing is not well-organized. ❏ It fits the writer's purpose somewhat.	❏ Some of the writing is smooth. Many sentences do not flow smoothly.
1	❏ The writing is not organized at all. ❏ It does not fit the writer's purpose.	❏ The sentences do not flow smoothly or logically.

Writing Project: Prewrite

Idea Web

Complete the idea web for your photo essay.

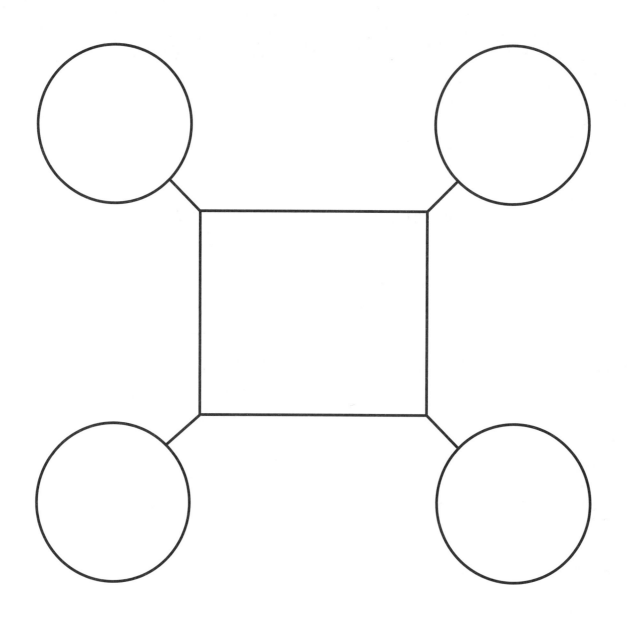

Name _____ Date _____

Revise

Use the Revising Marks to revise this paragraph. Look for:

- parts of a photo essay
- pictures and sentences that match
- details that relate to the topic
- proper nouns that use capital letters

Revising Marks	
∧	Add.
⅌	Take out.
⬭⌒	Move to here.
＝	Capitalize.

My family loves colorado.

Aunt Maggie lives in Denver. She works in an office.

I have to wear lots of clothes to stay warm.

We go skiing.

Name _____   Date _____

Edit and Proofread

Use the Editing Marks to edit and proofread this essay. Look for:

- details that match the topic
- misspelled words with the letters *s, m, h, t,* and *a*
- correct use of plural nouns (*-s* and *-es*)
- a capital letter beginning each proper noun

Editing Marks	
∧	Add.
⌃	Take out.
⟳	Move to here.
◯	Check spelling.
≡	Capitalize.

The State Fair of Texas
By Matt Brown

We go to the state fair of texas every

summer. This my brother sam at the

ham stand.

This is my sister jan with the

man who does magic trickes.

Magik is easy to learn.

Name _____   Date _____

Shoot for the Sun

Make a concept map with the answers to the Big Question: When is something alive?

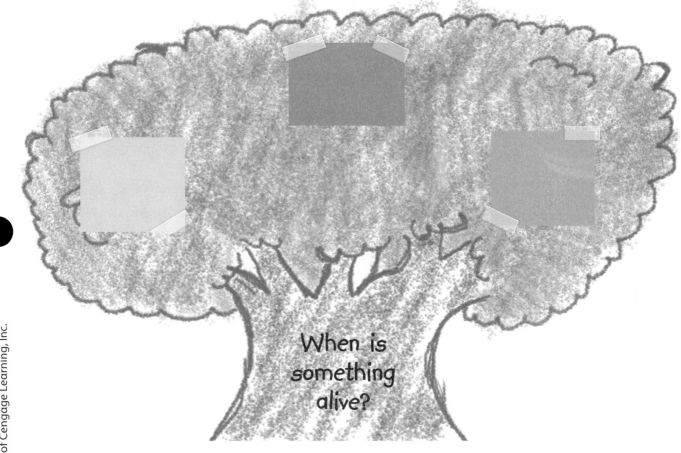

When is something alive?

Thinking Map: Checklist

List Facts

Use the checklist. Decide if the things in the pictures are living or nonliving. Add more items to the checklist.

Living Things Checklist	
can eat	☐
can drink	☐
is healthy	☐
can think	☐
	☐
	☐

Name _____   Date _____

Time for Dinner

Grammar Rules Adjectives: Color, Size, and Shape

1. An adjective describes, or tells about, a noun.
2. Some adjectives tell about color, size, or shape.

   My mom put the <u>big</u>, <u>purple</u> grapes in a <u>round</u> bowl.

Draw a line under the adjective. Write if the adjective tells about color, size, or shape.

1. My dad made a <u>big</u> dinner.  _size_

2. I set the square table. _____

3. This is a small piece of chicken. _____

4. We eat green vegetables. _____

5. The white potatoes are in the bowl. _____

6. I put the round dish in the sink. _____

💬 **Work with a partner. Make a list of adjectives that tell about color, size, and shape.**

Are You Living?

1

Living things eat and sleep. They breathe air. They move around.

2

Plants grow. They need damp ground and sunshine.

3

Living things fly and run. They need to drink and eat.

Grammar: Adjectives

How Many? How Much?

Grammar Rules Adjectives

- Use number words, such as *two*, to tell exactly how many things there are.

    Two plants have pink flowers.

- Use words, such as *much, some,* or *many*, when you don't know the exact number.

    There are many plants in the garden.

Draw a line under the adjective that tells how much or how many in each sentence. Then draw the picture on a seperate piece of paper.

1. Draw a picture of <u>two</u> people eating at a table.

2. Draw two plates on the table.

3. Draw a few muffins on the plates.

4. Draw a little milk in a glass.

 **Write a caption for your drawing. Use adjectives that tell how much or how many. Read your caption to a partner.**

Rivet

1. Write the first letter of each word.

2. Try to guess the word.

3. Fill in the other letters of the word.

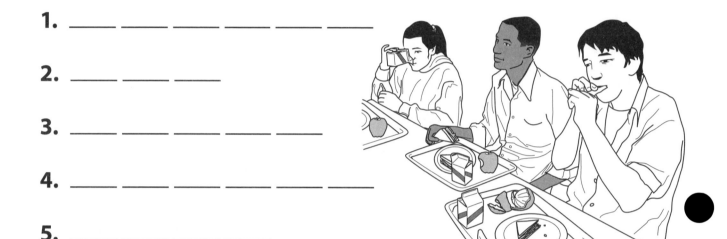

1. __ __ __ __ __ __ __

2. __ __ __ __

3. __ __ __ __ __ __ __ __

4. __ __ __ __ __ __ __ __

5. __ __ __ __ __

6. __ __ __ __ __ __ __ __ __

7. __ __ __ __ __ __

8. __ __ __ __ __ __ __

9. __ __ __ __ __

10. __ __ __ __ __ __ __ __ __ __

11. __ __ __ __ __ __ __ __ __ __

💬 **Take turns with a partner. Choose a word. Say it in a sentence.**

Name _____   Date _____

Reread and Describe: Checklist

Are You Living?

Add facts you learned about living things to the checklist. Place check marks in the boxes.

Living Things Checklist	
can eat	☑
can drink	☑
is healthy	☑
can think	☑
	☐
	☐
	☐
	☐

 Take turns with a partner. Tell a fact that you learned about living things in "Are You Living?"

For use with TE p. T87c   **2.7**   **Unit 2** | Shoot for the Sun

© National Geographic Learning, a part of Cengage Learning, Inc.

Name _____   Date _____

Are You Living?

Use this passage to practice reading with proper phrasing.

Living things need dinner,   4

Or they get much thinner.   9

So they need   12

To drink and feed.   16

Phrasing

B ☐ Rarely pauses while reading the text.   A ☐ Frequently pauses at appropriate points in the text.

I ☐ Occasionally pauses while reading the text.   AH ☐ Consistently pauses at all appropriate points in the text.

Accuracy and Rate Formula

Use the formula to measure a reader's accuracy and rate while reading aloud.

$$\underline{\hspace{3cm}} - \underline{\hspace{3cm}} = \underline{\hspace{3cm}}$$

| words attempted in one minute | number of errors | words correct per minute (wcpm) |

Respond and Extend: T Chart

Compare Genres

Compare a song and a diagram.

Song	Diagram
	has numbered steps

Work with a partner. Take turns asking about a song and a diagram.

Name _____   Date _____

Draw It!

Grammar Rules Adjectives

1. Adjectives describe how something looks.
2. Some adjectives tell about color, size, or shape.

The green plant is tall.

Read each sentence. Draw a line under each adjective. Then use the sentences to draw a picture on a separate piece on paper.

1. The park has green grass and yellow flowers.

2. Children play with a big, red ball.

3. A small, brown bird flies above.

4. A boy rides a blue bike with round wheels.

5. A tall man sells balloons in many shapes and sizes.

 Take turns with a partner. Show your picture and describe it.

© National Geographic Learning, a part of Cengage Learning, Inc.

Name _____ Date _____

Identify Plot

Retell a story you know to a partner. Fill out the chart.

Title: _____

Character:

Character:

Setting:

Plot:

Name _____   Date _____

I Spy

Grammar Rules Number Words

Numbers can be adjectives.

- Use number words to tell exactly how many things there are.

  Paulo gave <u>three</u> flowers to his mom.

Look at the picture next to each sentence. Count the things in the picture. Write the number in the sentence.

1. Justin picks ---- *two* ---- apples.

2. We saw _____ birds.

3. Lisa has _____ ball.

4. Rosa has _____ cats.

5. Dad read me _____ books.

Write two sentences about yourself using number words. Say them to a partner.

Key Points Reading

The Daisy

A seed sleeps under the Earth. The sun shines and the rain falls.

The sun knocks on the door and asks the seed to come out and play. The seed says she wants to sleep.

A raindrop knocks on the door and asks the seed to come out and play. The seed keeps sleeping.

Time passes. The sun and the rain knock on the seed's door. A leaf and a bud grow. Petals open. The daisy smiles. She is ready to play.

Grammar: Count and Noncount Words

My Puppy's Needs

Grammar Rules Count and Noncount Words

1. Count words name things that can be counted.

  • Use number words and other adjectives, such as *many*.

2. Noncount words name things that cannot be counted.

  • Use adjectives, such as *some* and *more*.

  I ate <u>one</u> banana and drank <u>some</u> milk.

1. Toss a marker onto one of the sentence parts below.

2. Find the other part that correctly completes the sentence. Say the complete sentence.

3. Take turns with a partner. The player who makes the most correct sentences wins.

My puppy, Spot, needs some	My dad takes Spot for three
legs.	water.
Spot eats a lot of	Spot has four
walks a day.	Spot has a few
food.	toys.

Vocabulary: Apply Word Knowledge

Around the World

1. The traveler stands behind a challenger.

2. Listen to the clue. Find the Key Word and say it.

3. The first to answer correctly travels to the next student on the right. The first traveler to go all around the circle wins.

Leaf!

KEY WORDS

seed	bud	petal	flower	leaf

CLUES

- a part of a plant that is the start of a flower

- the flat, green part of a plant

- the flat part of a flower

- a part of a plant that is small and grows into a new plant

- a part of a plant that has many petals

Name _____   Date _____

The Daisy

Complete the chart. Describe what happens to the little seed in "The Daisy."

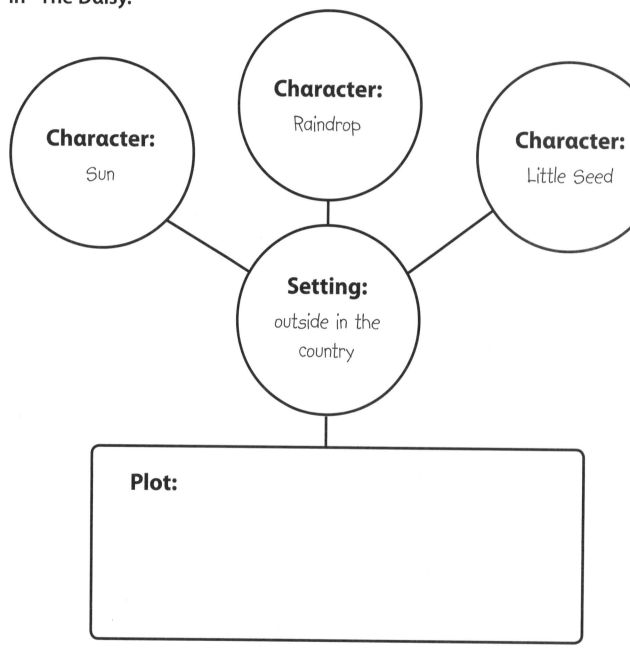

Character:
Sun

Character:
Raindrop

Character:
Little Seed

Setting:
outside in the country

Plot:

 Take turns with a partner. Use your chart to describe what happens to the little seed.

The Daisy

Use this passage to practice reading with proper phrasing.

Time passes. The sun rises. 5

More rain falls. 8

The sun and the rain knock on the 16

little seed's door. 19

Phrasing

| B | ☐ Rarely pauses while reading the text. | A | ☐ Frequently pauses at appropriate points in the text. |
| I | ☐ Occasionally pauses while reading the text. | AH | ☐ Consistently pauses at all appropriate points in the text. |

Accuracy and Rate Formula

Use the formula to measure a reader's accuracy and rate while reading aloud.

$$\underset{\substack{\text{words attempted}\\\text{in one minute}}}{\underline{\hspace{3cm}}} - \underset{\substack{\text{number of errors}}}{\underline{\hspace{3cm}}} = \underset{\substack{\text{words correct per minute}\\\text{(wcpm)}}}{\underline{\hspace{3cm}}}$$

Compare Genres

Compare a folk tale and a project notebook.

Folk Tale	Project Notebook
is a fantasy	is nonfiction

💬 **Take turns with a partner. Tell how a folk tale is different than a project notebook.**

Grammar: Adjectives

At School

Grammar Rules Adjectives

1. Some adjectives tell how many there are of something.

I ate <u>three</u> pears.

2. Some adjectives tell how much there is of something.

I need <u>some</u> water.

Complete the sentences below. Use words from the box.

much
some
five
many
ten

1. There are .... many .... books in the library.

2. There are .... soccer balls in the gym.

3. There is .... food in the cafeteria.

4. There is not .... milk in the cafeteria.

5. There are .... pencils on the desk.

💬 **Write two sentences about your school. Use adjectives. Read them to a partner.**

Writing Project: Rubric

Organization

	Is the writing well-organized? Does it fit the writer's purpose?	Does the writing flow?
4	❑ The writing is very well-organized. ❑ It clearly fits the writer's purpose.	❑ The writing is smooth and logical. Each sentence flows into the next one.
3	❑ Most of the writing is organized. ❑ It mostly fits the writer's purpose.	❑ Most of the writing is smooth. There are only a few sentences that do not flow logically.
2	❑ The writing is not well-organized. ❑ It fits the writer's purpose somewhat.	❑ Some of the writing is smooth. Many sentences do not flow smoothly.
1	❑ The writing is not organized at all. ❑ It does not fit the writer's purpose.	❑ The sentences do not flow smoothly or logically.

© National Geographic Learning, a part of Cengage Learning, Inc.

● Plan

Write the title of your how-to article.
Then plan your writing. Use a web.

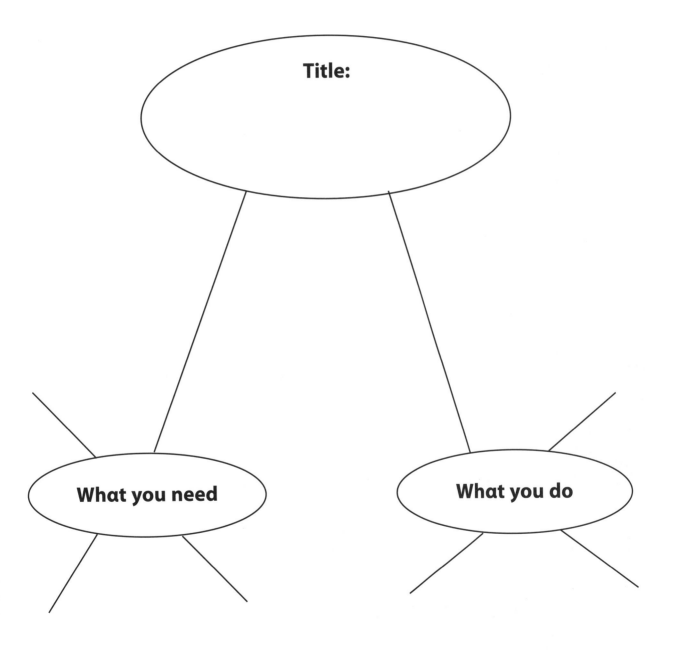

Writing Project

Revise

Use the Revising Marks to revise the how-to article. Look for:

- **the correct parts of a how-to article**
- **complete instructions**
- **steps that are in the right order (sequence)**
- **proper end punctuation**

Revising Marks	
∧	Add.
⌇	Take out.
⌒⌁	Move to here.

How to Make a Flower Bookmark

by Mari Lee

What You Need

brawing paper, book, scissors, colored paper,

What You Do

1. Fold drawing paper and put the flower inside it?

2. Put the paper and flower inside. Get a large book.

3. Glue the pressed flower onto the bookmark

4. Cut a bookmark from the colored paper.

Writing Project

Edit and Proofread

Use the Editing Marks to edit and proofread this how-to article.
Look for:

- **proper use of adjectives**
- **proper end punctuation**
- **misspelled words**

Editing Marks	
∧	Add.
┙	Take out.
⬯⌐	Move to here.
⬯	Check spelling.
⊙	Add a period.

How to Make a Plant Book

What You Need

pant

wax paper

book

What You Do

1. Pluck a plant.

2. Put it in wax paper

3. Put it in a book big.

4. In week, get the fat plant.

5. Gue the pant on back paper

6. Clip papers Make a book.

Unit Concept Map

To Your Front Door

Make a concept map with the answers to the Big Question: How do we get what we need?

How do we get what we need?

Name ______________________ Date ______________

Thinking Map: T Chart

Categorize Needs and Wants

List what you need and what you want in the T chart below.

Need	Want
• peas	• toy car
• fish	• ball
•	•
•	•
•	•

Grammar: Verbs

Shopping at the Market

Grammar Rules Verbs

A verb tells about the subject of the sentence.

Susan and Jamie <u>buy</u> apples.

Circle the verb in each sentence.

1. Dad and I (walk) to the market.

2. Dad and I shop for fish and peas.

3. Dad and I also buy apples and cheese.

4. Dad and I ride home on the bus.

5. Dad and I eat fish, peas, apples, and cheese for dinner.

💬 **Tell a partner what you do at the market.**

Key Points Reading

Markets

1

People shop at markets. Markets sell many different things. They sell food. They sell clothes.

2

There are many types of markets. They can be big or small. They are in many different places.

3

There are markets in many countries. Markets are special. People need markets.

Grammar: Action Verbs

Spin!

Grammar Rules Action Verbs

An action verb tells what someone or something does.

The boy <u>plays</u> the game.

1. Play with a partner.
2. Spin the spinner.
3. Use an action verb to tell what the person is doing in the picture.

Make a Spinner

1. Put a paper clip in the center of the circle.

2. Hold one end of the paper clip with a pencil.

3. Spin the paper clip around the pencil.

National Geographic Learning, a part of Cengage Learning, Inc.

Vocabulary: Apply Word Knowledge

Rivet

1. Write the first letter of each word.

2. Try to guess the word.

3. Fill in the other letters of the word.

1. _____ _____ _____ _____ _____

2. _____ _____ _____ _____ _____

3. _____ _____ _____ _____ _____ _____

4. _____ _____ _____ _____ _____

5. _____ _____ _____

6. _____ _____ _____ _____ _____ _____ _____

7. _____ _____ _____ _____ _____

8. _____ _____ _____

9. _____ _____ _____ _____

10. _____ _____ _____

Take turns with a partner. Choose a word. Say it in a sentence.

Markets

List types of markets that you read about. List what each market sells in the What It Sells column.

Type of Market	What It Sells
• fruit market	• bananas, pears, grapes
•	•
•	•
•	•

 Take turns with a partner. Tell what you learned about markets. Use your T chart.

Fluency: Intonation

Markets

Use this passage to practice reading with proper intonation.

Markets are special wherever   4

you go.   6

People need markets.   9

Intonation

| B | ☐ Does not change pitch. | A | ☐ Changes pitch to match some of the content. |
| I | ☐ Changes pitch, but does not match content. | AH | ☐ Changes pitch to match all of the content. |

Accuracy and Rate Formula

Use the formula to measure a reader's accuracy and rate while reading aloud.

$$\underline{\hspace{3cm}} - \underline{\hspace{3cm}} = \underline{\hspace{3cm}}$$

words attempted   number of errors   words correct per
in one minute   minute (wcpm)

Compare Author's Purpose

Compare the authors' purposes in the social studies and online articles.

	Markets	Flower Power
Topic	markets around the world	
Author's Purpose		

 Tell a partner how the authors' purposes in the social studies and online articles are alike and different.

Name _____   Date _____

From Farm to Market

Grammar Rules Present Tense Verbs

Tell what one person or thing does now.	Use *s* at the end of the verb.

Marta sells fruit.

Read each sentence. Circle the correct word. Write the word.

1. The farmer <u>grows</u> flowers.
   grow
   (grows)

2. Leo and Rita _____ flowers.
   grow
   grows

3. The woman _____ flowers.
   sell
   sells

4. Kyle and Eva _____ flowers.
   sell
   sells

5. Mom _____ flowers.
   buy
   buys

6. Andy and Jorge _____ flowers.
   buy
   buys

 Make a list of verbs with a partner. Write a sentence with one verb for your partner to read aloud.

Thinking Map: Idea Web

Identify Details

Complete the Idea Web. Place one answer to the question in each circle.

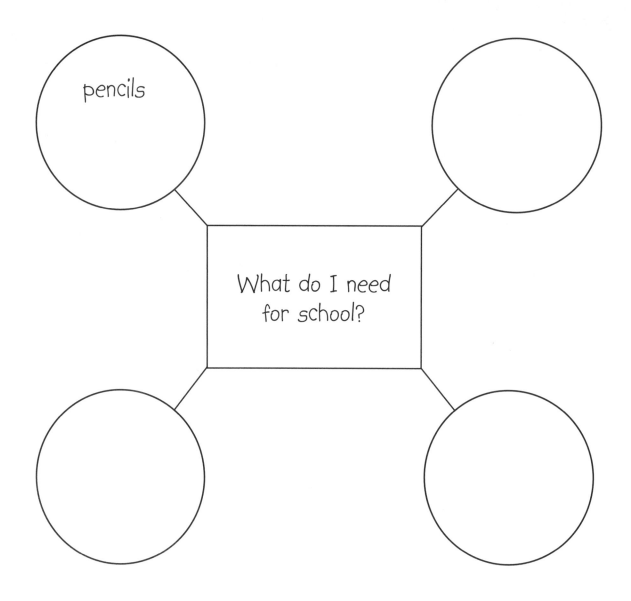

3.11

onal Geographic Learning, a part of Cengage Learning, Inc.

Name _____ Date _____

My Neighborhood

Grammar Rules Verbs: *to be*

Some verbs tell what a subject of a sentence is or is like.

Subject	*To be*
I	Use *am*.
a boy, a girl, or a thing	Use *is*.
more than one person or thing	Use *are*.

Complete each sentence. Write *am*, *is*, or *are*.

1. This _____is_____ is my neighborhood.

2. It _____ busy.

3. There _____ stores and markets.

4. Lynn _____ my neighbor.

5. My neighbors _____ friendly.

6. I _____ happy to live here.

💬 **Tell a partner about your neighborhood. Use a form of *be*.**

3.12

Key Points Reading

Delivery

1

A new day begins.

2

Trucks and vans deliver papers, boxes, and cans. Airplanes carry people and things.

3

Trucks and trains carry loads. Ships carry containers.

4

A new day begins. Delivery!

Grammar: Verbs: *to have*

One, Two, Three

Grammar Rules Verbs: *to have*

Some verbs tell what the subject of a sentence has.

Subject	*To have*
I or more than one person or thing	Use *have*.
one person or thing	Use *has*.

1. **Choose a word in Row 1.**
2. **Choose the verb that matches in Row 2.**
3. **Complete the sentence with a phrase from Row 3.**
4. **Take turns with a partner.**

Row 1			
Marcus	I	Julio and Sara	Karen
Row 2			
has	has	have	have
Row 3			
a truck.	a plane.	a train.	a van.

 Read your sentences to a partner.

Vocabulary: Apply Word Knowledge

Vocabulary Bingo

1. Write Key Words on the lines.

2. Listen to the clues. Place a marker on the Key Word.

3. Say "Bingo" when you have four markers in a row.

_____ _____ _____ _____

_____ _____ _____ _____

_____ _____ _____ _____

_____ _____ _____ _____

Reread and Retell: Idea Web

Delivery

Complete the Idea Web using details from "Delivery."

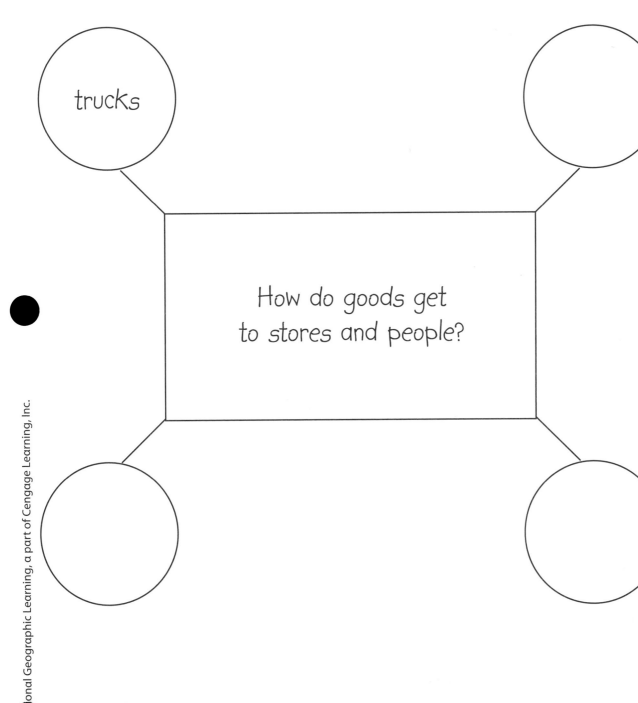

trucks

How do goods get
to stores and people?

💬 **Use your Idea Web to retell the poem to a partner.**

Name _____ Date _____

Delivery

Use this passage to practice reading with proper intonation.

A new day is on its way.

Delivery!

7

8

Intonation

B ☐ Does not change pitch.	A ☐ Changes pitch to match some of the content.
I ☐ Changes pitch, but does not match content.	AH ☐ Changes pitch to match all of the content.

Accuracy and Rate Formula

Use the formula to measure a reader's accuracy and rate while reading aloud.

$$\underline{\hspace{3cm}} - \underline{\hspace{3cm}} = \underline{\hspace{3cm}}$$

| words attempted in one minute | number of errors | words correct per minute (wcpm) |

Name _____   Date _____

Respond and Extend: T Chart

Compare Genres

Compare a poem and a fact sheet.

Poem	Fact Sheet
has illustrations or pictures	has photographs

 Tell a partner how a poem and a fact sheet are different. Use your T chart.

Name _____   Date _____

Who Is? Who Has?

Grammar Rules Subject-Verb Agreement

Subject	To be	To have
one person or thing	is	has
more than one person or thing	are	have

Look at each picture below. Choose the correct verb in ( ) and write it on the line.

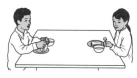

1. This ___is___ Tim. (is, are)

2. Lara _____ a cart. (have, has)

3. The children _____ hungry. (is, are)

4. Max and Sue _____ food. (have, has)

5. Max and Sue _____ full. (am, are)

Choose a form of *be* or *have*. Ask a partner to say a sentence using it.

Name _____   Date _____

Ideas

	Is the message clear and focused?	Do the details show the writer knows the topic?
4	❏ All of the writing is clear and focused.	❏ All the details tell about the topic. The writer knows the topic well.
3	❏ Most of the writing is clear and focused.	❏ Most of the details are about the topic. The writer knows the topic fairly well.
2	❏ Some of the writing is not clear. The writing lacks some focus.	❏ Some details are about the topic. The writer doesn't know the topic well.
1	❏ The writing is not clear or focused.	❏ Many details are not about the topic. The writer does not know the topic.

Writing Project: Prewrite

Idea Web

Complete the idea web for your thank you letter.

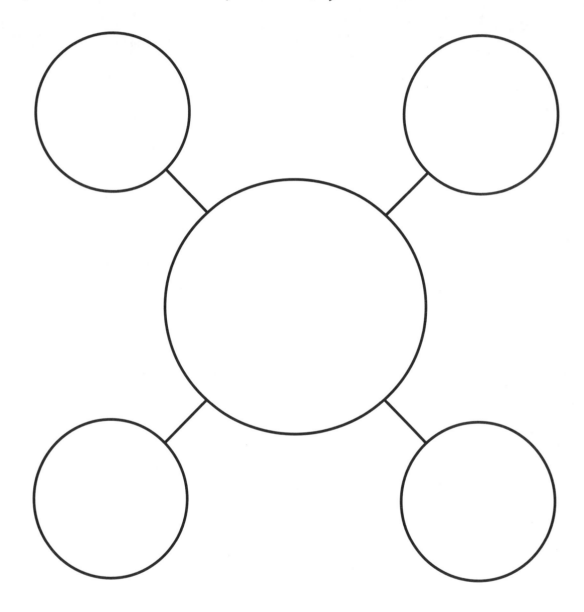

Name ______________________ Date ______________

Writing Project

Revise

Use the Revising Marks to revise this paragraph. Look for:

- **a good topic sentence**
- **complete sentences**
- **correct subject-verb agreement**

Revising Marks	
∧	Add.
	Take out.
	Move to here.

May 3

Dear Dad,

Thank you. I love him because he are so fun! wanted a puppy for a long time. I needed a friend to play with in the park. We has lots of fun together there, and I are so happy.

Love,

Casey

Writing Project

Edit and Proofread

Use the Editing Marks to edit and
proofread this paragraph. Look for:

- **subject-verb agreement**
- **correct capital letters at the
  beginning of each sentence**
- **correctly-written letters
  (no backwards letters)**

Editing Marks	
∧	Add.
ℛ	Take out.
⬭⌐	Move to here.
⬭	Check spelling.
≡	Capitalize.

June 6

Dear Grandma,

a book are the best gift. Love dooks. some kibs reads books

about airqlanes or sports stars. Other kids has books about animals

or adventures. if you wants to give a great gift, give a book!

Love,

Eric

Name _____   Date _____

Unit Concept Map

Growing and Changing

Make a concept map with the answers to the Big Question: How do animals change as they grow?

How do animals change as they grow?

National Geographic Learning, a part of Cengage Learning, Inc.

Identify Plot

Think of a story you know. Write or draw the plot in the chart.

Beginning:

Middle:

End:

Name _____   Date _____

Grammar: Singular Subject Pronouns

Who Is It?

Grammar Rules Singular Subject Pronouns

Use *I* for yourself.	I *see a duck.*
Use *you* when you talk to one person.	You *see a duck.*
Use *it* for one place or thing.	It *is in the pond.*

Circle the pronoun in each sentence.

1. (You) see the nest.

2. It is in the bush.

3. I want to see the eggs.

4. You hope the eggs hatch soon.

5. It is hatching!

Choose one pronoun used above. Write a new sentence. Read it to a parter.

Ruby in Her Own Time

1  A mother and father duck live on a nest. There are five eggs in the nest. The mother duck sits on the eggs.

2 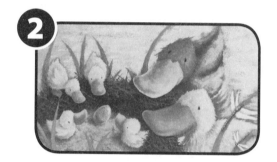 Four eggs hatch. The fifth egg does nothing. Father Duck asks if it will ever hatch. Mother Duck says it will in its own time. It does.

3  Ruby's brothers and sisters eat, swim, and grow. Ruby does too, in her own time.

4  Ruby's brothers and sisters fly. Ruby flies away. Mother Duck asks if she will ever come back. Father Duck says she will, in her own time. She does.

Grammar: Plural Subject Pronouns

The Pond

Grammar Rules Plural Subject Pronouns

Use *we* for yourself and another person.	<u>Dan and I</u> saw a duck. <u>We</u> saw a duck.
Use *you* when you talk to one person or more.	<u>You and Scott</u> saw a duck. <u>You</u> saw a duck.
Use *they* to talk about more than one person.	<u>Allison and Rachel</u> saw a duck. <u>They</u> saw a duck.

Read the sentences. Write a pronoun for the underlined words. Use *We*, *You*, or *They*.

1. <u>Max, Pete, and I</u> went to the pond. _____ We _____ saw a frog.

2. <u>You and Pete</u> saw ducks. _____ saw a duck's nest.

3. <u>Max and Pete</u> saw a fish. _____ saw it swimming.

4. <u>Pete and I</u> like the pond. _____ want to go again.

 Use the pronouns above. Tell a partner about your family.

Vocabulary: Apply Word Knowledge

Vocabulary Bingo

1. Write a Key Word in each egg.

2. Listen to the clues. Place a marker on the Key Word.

3. Say "Bingo" when you have four markers in a row.

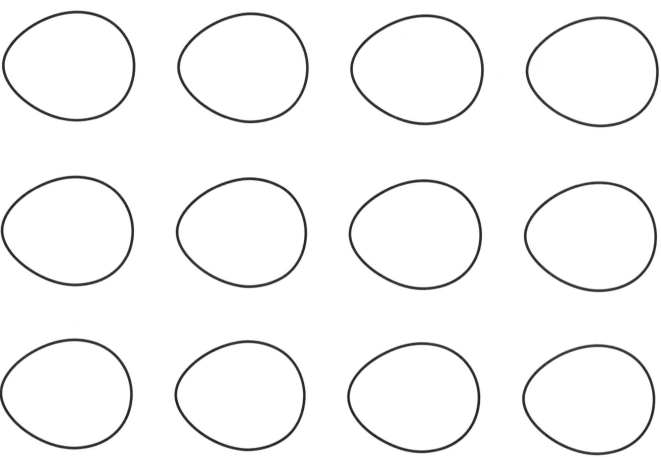

4.6

Name _____ Date _____

Ruby in Her Own Time

Complete the chart. Write the important parts of the plot from the story.

Beginning:

First, Ruby hatches from an egg.

Middle:

End:

 Use your chart to retell the story. Act out the events in order to a partner.

National Geographic Learning, a part of Cengage Learning, Inc.

Name _____   Date _____

Ruby in Her Own Time

Use this passage to practice reading with proper expression.

"Will she ever eat?" asked   5

Father Duck.   7

"She will," said Mother Duck,   12

"in her own time."   16

Expression

| B | ☐ Does not read with feeling. | A | ☐ Reads with appropriate feeling for most content. |
| I | ☐ Reads with some feeling, but does not match content. | AH | ☐ Reads with appropriate feeling for all content. |

Accuracy and Rate Formula

Use the formula to measure a reader's accuracy and rate while reading aloud.

_____ − _____ = _____
words attempted   number of errors   words correct per
 in one minute   minute (wcpm)

Respond and Extend: Venn Diagram

Compare Genres
Compare a story and a science article.

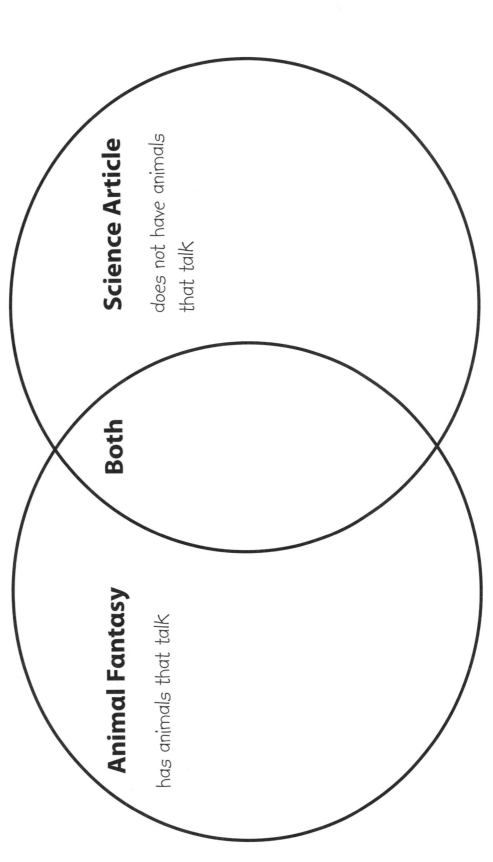

Science Article

does not have animals
that talk

Both

Animal Fantasy

has animals that talk

Tell a partner how a story and a science article are different. Then tell how they are the same.

Name _____   Date _____

The Make-It-a-Pronoun Game

Grammar Rules Subject Pronouns

Use *I* for yourself.	I draw a turtle.
Use *he* for a male.	Jun draws a turtle. He draws a turtle
Use *she* for a female.	Aida draws a turtle. She draws a turtle.
Use *they* for more than one person.	Jun and Aida draw turtles. They draw turtles.

1. **Play with a partner.**
2. **Spin the spinner.**
3. **Change the noun to a subject pronoun.**

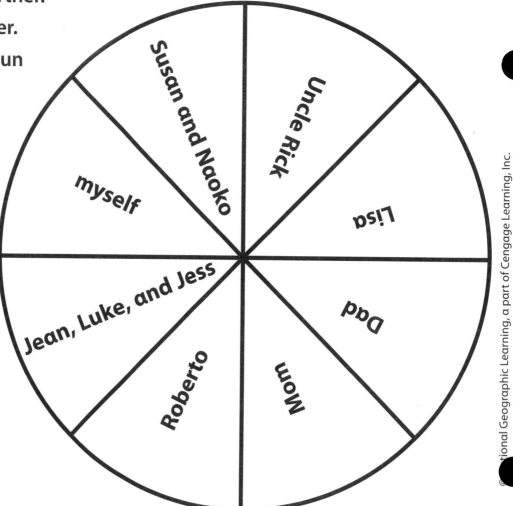

Make a Spinner

1. Put a paper clip ⊂⊃ in the center of the circle.

2. Hold one end of the paper clip with a pencil.

3. Spin the paper clip around the pencil.

Name _____   Date _____

Identify Main Idea and Details

Choose an animal. Write details about how the animal changes as it grows.

Main Idea: _____ change as they grow.
Detail:
Detail:
Detail:

Name _____   Date _____

My Pet

Grammar Rules Singular Possessive Words

A possessive word tells who owns or has something.
- Use *my* for I.
- Use *your* for *you*.
- Use *its* for an animal or a thing.

I have a frog. It is my frog.

**Complete each sentence with the correct possessive words.
Use *my, your,* or *its*.**

1. I have a dog. It is  dog.

2. You have a fish. It is -------------- fish.

3. I have a cat. It is ---------------- cat.

4. This cat has a tail. ---------------- tail is long.

5. You have a rabbit. It is ---------------- rabbit.

**Say sentences with a partner. Tell about things in your classroom.
Use *my, your,* and *its*.**

Name _____   Date _____

A Butterfly is Born

A butterfly
lays an egg.

A caterpillar hatches.

The butterfly
flies away.

The pupa becomes
a butterfly.

The caterpillar
makes a chrysalis.

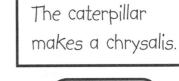

The caterpillar
becomes a pupa.

Who Owns It?

Grammar Rules Plural Possessive Words

A possessive word tells who owns or has something.
- Use *our* for *we*.
- Use *their* for *they* or more than one.

We live in a house. This is our home.
The frogs live in a pond. That is their home.

1. Toss a marker onto one of the sentence parts below.

2. Put it together with another sentence part. The noun or pronoun should match the possessive word.

3. Write the complete sentence on a separate piece of paper.

4. Say the sentence to your partner.

put on their hats.	**They**
We	**Lisa and Alexis**
do our homework.	**read their books.**
Juan and I	**eat our lunch.**

4.14

Vocabulary: Apply Word Knowledge

Yes or No?

1. **Listen to the questions. Write the Key Word where it belongs in each sentence.**
2. **Listen to the questions again.**
3. **Check *yes* or *no* for each question.**

		yes	no

1. Can a _____ hang from a leaf?   ☐ ☐

2. Does a _____ stay the same as it grows?   ☐ ☐

3. Can a _____ fly?   ☐ ☐

4. Does a _____ lay eggs?   ☐ ☐

5. Does every _____ have wings?   ☐ ☐

6. Will you _____ as you grow?   ☐ ☐

Reread and Summarze: Main Idea and Details Chart

A Butterfly is Born

Write details in the chart that tell how a caterpillar changes into a butterfly.

Main Idea:
A caterpillar changes into a butterfly.

Detail:
hatches from an egg
Detail:
Detail:
Detail:
Detail:
Detail:

 Summarize what you learned about a butterfly's life to a partner. Use your Main Idea and Details Chart.

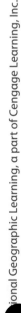
...ional Geographic Learning, a part of Cengage Learning, Inc.

Fluency: Phrasing

A Butterfly Is Born

Use this passage to practice reading with proper phrasing.

The butterfly is tired. Its wings   6

are wet. It rests and dries.   12

The butterfly flies away.   16

Expression

| B | ☐ Rarely pauses while reading the text. | A | ☐ Frequently pauses at appropriate points in the text. |
| I | ☐ Occasionally pauses while reading the text. | AH | ☐ Consistently pauses at all appropriate points in the text. |

Accuracy and Rate Formula

Use the formula to measure a reader's accuracy and rate while reading aloud.

$$\underline{\hspace{3cm}} - \underline{\hspace{3cm}} = \underline{\hspace{3cm}}$$

words attempted   number of errors   words correct per
in one minute   minute (wcpm)

National Geographic Learning, a part of Cengage Learning, Inc.

Compare Genres

Compare a science article and a poem.

Science Article	Poem
has real information	has information that is not real

💬 **Tell a partner how a science article and a poem are different.**

© National Geographic Learning, a part of Cengage Learning, Inc.

Grammar: Possessive Words

His or Her?

Grammar Rules Possessive Words

| Use *her* for one girl or one woman. | Mom grows flowers in her garden. |
| Use *his* for one boy or one man. | Dad uses his garden tools. |

Read each sentence. Circle the correct possessive word. Write the sentence.

1. Kate writes about (his/**her**) pet.

   Kate writes about her pet.

2. Mark tells about (his /her) frog.

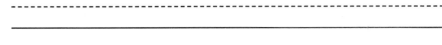

3. Dad has (his /her) pen to draw.

4. Grandma is in (his/ her) garden.

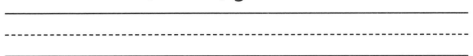

5. Anita reads (his/ her) book.

Write a new sentence with *his* or *her*. Read it to a partner.

Writing Project: Rubric

Voice

	Does the tone, formal or informal, fit the purpose and audience?	Does the writing sound genuine to the writer?
4	❑ The writer's tone fits the purpose and audience.	❑ The writing is genuine. It shows who the writer is.
3	❑ The writer's tone mostly fits the purpose and audience.	❑ Most of the writing sounds genuine.
2	❑ Some of the writing fits the purpose and audience. Some does not.	❑ Some of the writing sounds genuine.
1	❑ The writer's tone does not fit the purpose and audience.	❑ The writing does not sound genuine.

Name ______________________ Date ____________

Writing Project: Prewrite

Beginning-Middle-End Chart

Complete the chart for your story.

Beginning:
↓
Middle:
↓
End:

Writing Project

Revise

Use the Revising Marks to revise this paragraph. Look for:

- **a beginning, middle, and end**
- **words that could sound more like you or be more interesting**

Revising Marks	
∧	Add.
℘	Take out.
⬯⌐	Move to here.

First, we made the crust. I helped roll it out and put it in the pie pan.

I learned how to bake a pie from my grandmother. Then, we made the

filling. I helped slice the apples and add the sugar. It was good.

Writing Project

Edit and Proofread

Use the Editing Marks to edit and proofread this paragraph. Look for:

- **correct subject and possessive pronouns**
- **correct capital letters for the pronoun "I"**
- **correct spelling errors: words that sound alike but are spelled differently**

Editing Marks	
∧	Add.
ℱ	Take out.
⬭⌒	Move to here.
⬭	Check spelling.
≡	Capitalize.

My friend Ike and her sister Tina learned to swim this year. i

already new how to swim, so i helped them. First, Ike tried to swim,

but he was scared. Then, Tina started to swim, two. They wasn't

scared at all. Finally, Tina and i helped Ike until he learned. Now

Ike likes to swim in his pool.

National Geographic Learning, a part of Cengage Learning, Inc.

Name _____ Date _____

Creature Features

Make a concept map with the answers to the Big Question: How are animals different?

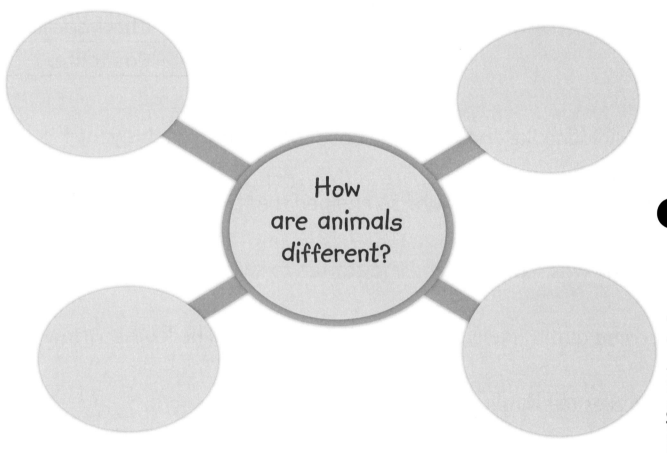

5.1

Name _____   Date _____

Thinking Map: Venn Diagram

Compare and Contrast Animals

Choose two animals. Compare and contrast the animals in the Venn diagram.

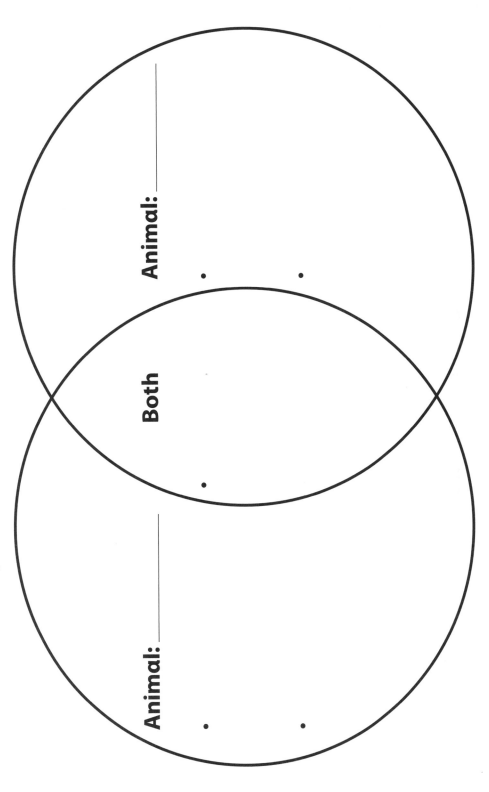

Animal: _____

Both

Animal: _____

5.2

Grammar: Sentences

Name that Part

Grammar Rules Sentences

A sentence has a **naming part** and a **telling part**.

(The bear) swims.

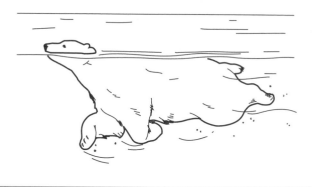

Circle the naming parts. Underline the telling parts.

1. (The dog) <u>barks</u>.

2. A bird sings.

3. My cat runs.

4. The alligator walks.

5. A rabbit hops.

 Choose one of the naming parts above. Add a telling part. Read your sentence to a partner.

Key Points Reading

For Pete's Sake

1

Pete was green. He wanted to be pink like everyone else. The others told him he just wasn't ripe yet.

2

Pete had four feet and no feathers. Everyone else had two feet and feathers. Nothing could make Pete feel happy.

3

Then some strangers arrived. They looked like Pete. He felt very happy.

4

Pete told the others he was different. He was the same, too. They told him that he always had been.

Name _____ Date _____

Can You See It?

Grammar Rules Sentence Capitalization

1. Sentences begin with a (capital) (letter.)
2. Sentences end with an end mark.

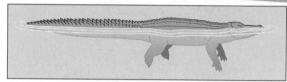

(The) alligator swims.

Read the group of words. Write each group as a sentence.
Use a capital letter and a period.

1. i see an alligator

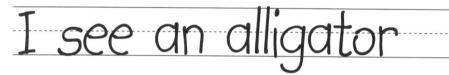

I see an alligator

2. it has scales

_____

- -

_____

3. it hides in tall grass

_____

- -

_____

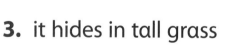 Read one of the sentences. Ask a partner to point to the capital
letter and end mark.

Vocabulary: Apply Word Knowledge

Vocabulary Bingo

1. Write Key Words.

2. Listen to the clues. Place a marker on the Key Word.

3. Say "Bingo" when you have four markers in a row.

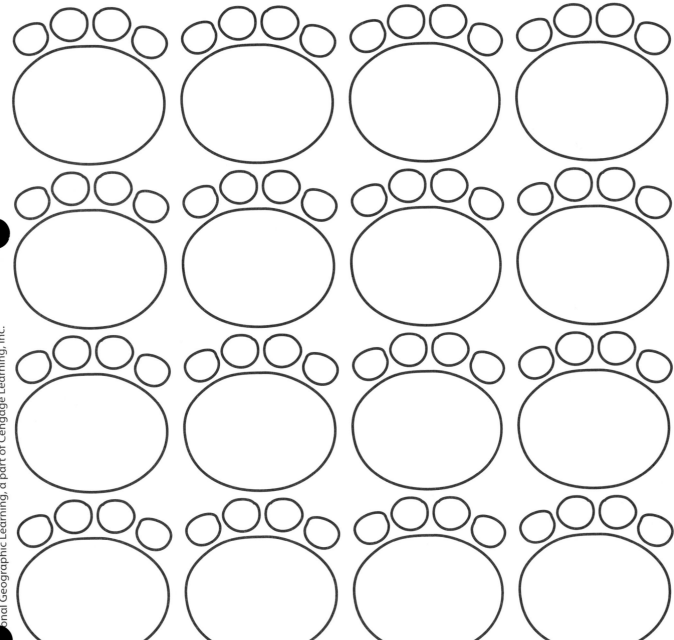

5.6

Name _____   Date _____

For Pete's Sake

Compare Pete and Pete's friends.

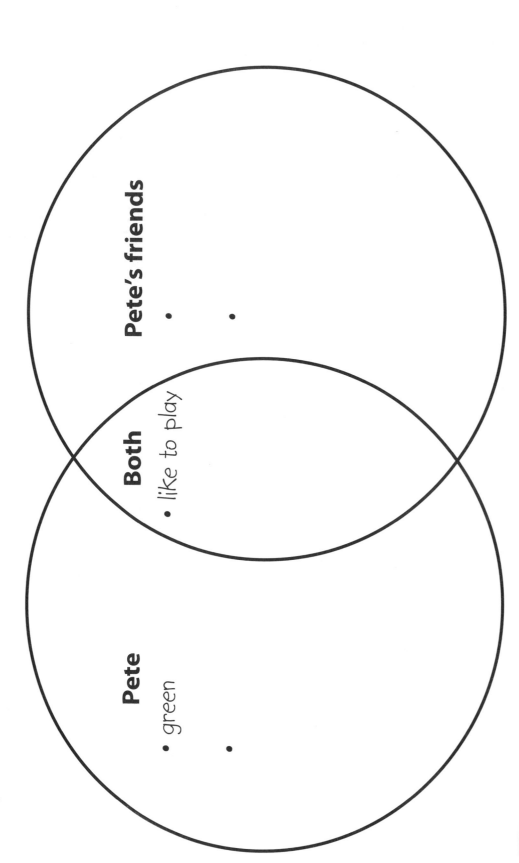

Pete
- green
- •

Both
- like to play

Pete's friends
- •
- •

Take turns with a partner. Tell about Pete and Pete's friends. Use your Venn diagram.

© National Geographic Learning, a part of Cengage Learning, Inc.

Fluency: Expression

For Pete's Sake

Use this passage to practice reading with proper expression.

"Stop!" said the others, laughing.   5

"You're getting our feathers wet."   10

Uh-oh. Pete didn't have any feathers.   16

National Geographic Learning, a part of Cengage Learning, Inc.

Expression

| B | ☐ Does not read with feeling. | A | ☐ Reads with appropriate feeling for most content. |

| I | ☐ Reads with some feeling, but does not match content. | AH | ☐ Reads with appropriate feeling for all content. |

Accuracy and Rate Formula

Use the formula to measure a reader's accuracy and rate while reading aloud.

$$\underline{\hspace{3cm}} - \underline{\hspace{3cm}} = \underline{\hspace{3cm}}$$

| words attempted in one minute | number of errors | words correct per minute (wcpm) |

Name ______________________ Date ______________

Respond and Extend: T Chart

Compare Genres

Compare a story and a science article.

Animal Fantasy	Science Article
no labels	has labels

Tell a partner how a story and a science article are different.

Grammar: Complete Sentences

Build a Sentence Game

Grammar Rules Complete Sentences

A complete sentence has a naming part and a telling part.

- Start a sentence with a (capital letter)
- End a sentence with an end mark.

Ⓐ tiger has paws.

1. Toss a marker onto one of the sentence parts below.

2. Put it together with another sentence part to make a complete sentence.

3. Write the complete sentence on a separate piece of paper.

4. Say the sentence to your partner.

the monkey	the elephant
has a tail	the giraffe
can run	has fur
can climb	the tiger
the snake	has a mouth

Categorize Movements

Add animals and their movements to the Category Chart.

Animals	Movement
fish turtle	swim
	fly
	run

Name _____   Date _____

Kit the Cat

Grammar Rules Simple Subject

1. The naming part of a sentence is called the <u>subject</u> of the sentence.

2. The <u>subject</u> tells who or what the sentence is about.

   <u>The bird</u> hops. <u>It</u> sings a song.

Circle the naming part in each sentence.

1. (The cat) naps.

2. It rests.

3. The puppy plays.

4. Kit wakes up.

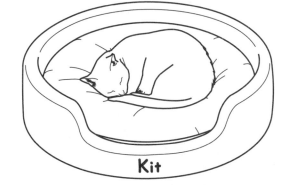

Kit

5. They run and jump.

 Choose a sentence above. Change the naming part. Say the new sentence to a partner.

National Geographic Learning, a part of Cengage Learning, Inc.

Key Points Reading

Slither, Slide, Hop, and Run

1 Birds fly through the air on wings. Snakes slither from side to side on the ground.

2 Horses run. They move their legs forward and backward. Kangaroos hop. They use their back feet. Snails slide slowly on the ground.

3 Dolphins swim. They move their tails up and down. Dogs dig. They move dirt with their paws. Raccoons climb. They move their feet up and down.

National Geographic Learning, a part of Cengage Learning, Inc.

Grammar: Simple Predicate

Match Sentence Parts

Grammar Rules Simple Predicate

1. The telling part of a sentence is called the predicate of the sentence.

2. The predicate can tell what the subject does.

The kitten <u>sits</u>.

1. Match a naming part with a telling part to make a sentence.

2. Write the sentence on a separate piece of paper. Circle the telling part.

The cat	The puppy
can run.	The monkey
jumps.	can swim.
is happy.	She
looks.	A dog

 Read one of your sentences to a partner. Say the telling part.

National Geographic Learning, a part of Cengage Learning, Inc.

Vocabulary: Apply Word Knowledge

Rivet

1. **Write the first letter of each word.**

2. **Try to guess the word.**

3. **Fill in the other letters of the word.**

1. ____ ____ ____ ____

2. ____ ____ ____ ____

3. ____ ____ ____ ____ ____ ____ ____ ____

4. ____ ____ ____

5. ____ ____ ____

6. ____ ____ ____ ____ ____

7. ____ ____ ____ ____ ____

8. ____ ____ ____

9. ____ ____ ____ ____

10. ____ ____ ____ ____ ____

11. ____ ____ ____ ____ ____ ____

Name _____ Date _____

Slither, Slide, Hop, and Run

Categorize the animals and their movements in "Slither, Slide, Hop, and Run."

Animals	Movement
birds bats	fly
horses	

 Use your Category Chart to summarize the information in the selection. Work with a partner.

Name _____   Date _____

Slither, Slide, Hop, and Run

Use this passage to practice reading with proper intonation.

A kangaroo can hop! It makes short   7

leaps into the air. It uses its back feet   16

to hop.   18

A horse can run! Its legs move forward   26

and backward very quickly.   30

Intonation

| B | ☐ Does not change pitch. | A | ☐ Changes pitch to match some of the content. |
| I | ☐ Changes pitch, but does not match content. | AH | ☐ Changes pitch to match all of the content. |

Accuracy and Rate Formula

Use the formula to measure a reader's accuracy and rate while reading aloud.

_____	−	_____	=	_____
words attempted in one minute		number of errors		words correct per minute (wcpm)

Respond and Extend: Venn Diagram

Compare Genres

Compare a fact book and a photo journal.

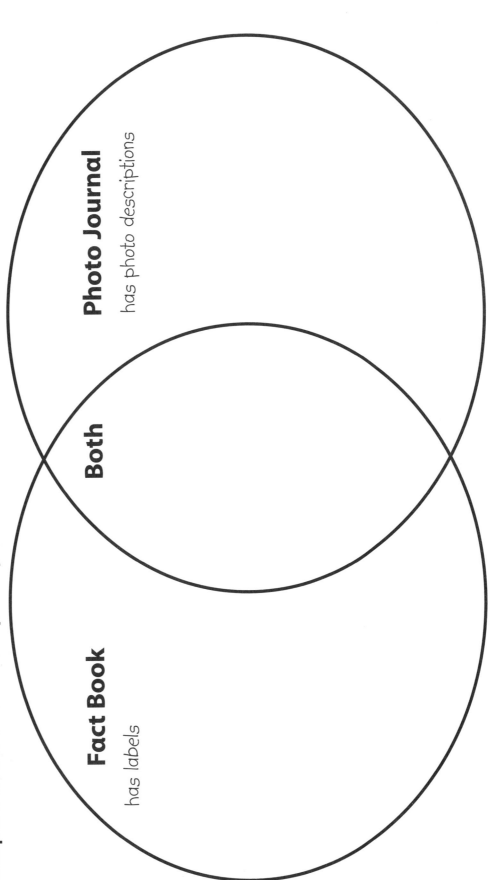

Photo Journal

has photo descriptions

Both

Fact Book

has labels

Tell a partner how a fact book and a photo journal are the same. Then tell how they are different.

Name _____ Date _____

Let's Swim

Grammar Rules Subject-Verb Agreement

1. If the subject names one, use *s* at the end of the verb.
2. If the subject names more than one, do not use *s* at the end of the verb.

Choose the verb that goes with the subject. Write the sentence.

1. One fish (swim/swims).

One fish swims.

2. Two fish (swim/swims).

3. A fish (come/comes) here.

4. Many fish (come/comes) here.

 Pick a verb from above. Write a new sentence. Read it to a partner.

National Geographic Learning, a part of Cengage Learning, Inc.

Name _____   Date _____

Voice

	Does the tone, formal or informal, fit the purpose and audience?	Does the writing sound genuine to the writer?
4	❑ The writer's tone fits the purpose and audience.	❑ The writing is genuine. It shows who the writer is.
3	❑ The writer's tone mostly fits the purpose and audience.	❑ Most of the writing sounds genuine.
2	❑ Some of the writing fits the purpose and audience. Some does not.	❑ Some of the writing sounds genuine.
1	❑ The writer's tone does not fit the purpose and audience.	❑ The writing does not sound genuine.

National Geographic Learning, a part of Cengage Learning, Inc.

Main Idea and Details Chart

Complete the Main Idea and Details Chart for your article.

Main Idea:

Supporting Detail:

Supporting Detail:

Supporting Detail:

Revise

Use the Revising Marks to revise this paragraph. Look for:

- **a main idea**
- **details that tell more about the main idea**
- **complete sentences**

Revising Marks	
∧	Add.
⌁	Take out.
⌀‾∧	Move to here.

A lion is the loudest cat ever. Its roar is heard mostly at night.

My favorite cat is the cheetah. A lion's roar can be heard from miles

away. Loud cat Dogs are loud, too.

Name ______________________ Date ______________

Writing Project

Edit and Proofread

Use the Revising Marks to edit and proofread this paragraph. Look for:

- **complete sentences**
- **subject-verb agreement**
- **capitalization and end punctuation**
- **correct spelling of long vowel words with silent *e***

Editing Marks	
^	Add.
℘	Take out.
⊂⊃→	Move to here.
◯	Check spelling.
≡	Capitalize.
⊙	Add a period.

grizzly bears sleeps all winter. First, they dig a den Then they crawl in and go to slep. Like to sleep!

Unit Concept Map

Up in the Air

Make a concept map with the answers to the Big Question: What's wild about weather?

Thinking Map: Cause-and-Effect Chart

Find Cause and Effect

Explain what happens when it rains all day. Write the effects in the Cause-and-Effect Chart.

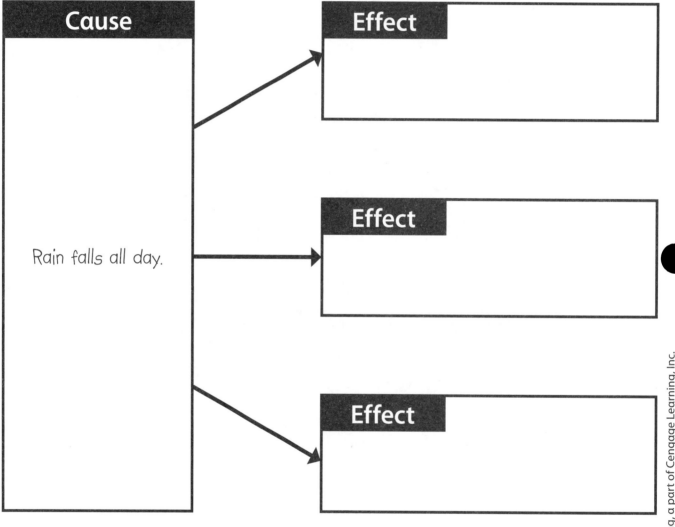

Cause		Effect

Rain falls all day.

Effect

Effect

© National Geographic Learning, a part of Cengage Learning, Inc.

Grammar: Statements, Exclamations, and Commands

Weather Report

Grammar Rules Statements, Exclamations, and Commands

Sentence Type	What It Does	How It Ends
statement	tells something	.
exclamation	tells something with strong feeling	!
command	tells someone to do something	. or !

1. With a partner, read the sentences.
2. Write *statement, exclamation,* or *command* next to each sentence.
3. The first pair to complete the activity correctly wins.

1. It is stormy.

statement

2. Bring your umbrella.

_____

3. It is very wet!

_____

4. It is windy.

_____

 Take turns with a partner. Say the sentences.

Name _____ Date _____

I Face the Wind

1  The wind is very strong. You can't see it but you can feel it. You can see what it does to flags, trees, and other things.

2  You can catch the air. You can make your own wind, too.

3  The wind is made of air. The fastest winds are called tornadoes. The softest winds are your breath. Face the wind. Feel it push you.

© National Geographic Learning, a part of Cengage Learning, Inc.

Name _____   Date _____

No, He Is Not

Grammar Rules Negative Sentences/Questions

Some questions can be answered with *yes* or *no*.

- Start these questions with *do, does, is, are,* or *can*.
- Use *no* and *not* for a negative answer.

  <u>Are</u> you ten years old?

  <u>No,</u> I am <u>not</u> ten years old.

Read the question. Look at the pictures. Then answer the question.

1. Is he wearing a hat?

No, he is not wearing a hat.

2. Does he have a coat?

_____

_____

3. Is she wearing a sweater?

_____

_____

4. Can she see snow?

_____

_____

💬 **Ask a partner a question about one of the pictures. Have your partner give a negative answer.**

Vocabulary: Apply Word Knowledge

Picture It

1. Form pairs. Choose a pair to be the artists and a pair to be the guessers.

2. The artists secretly select a Key Word.

3. The artists draw a picture to show the word's meaning.

4. The guessers guess what Key Word the picture shows.

5. Switch roles.

weather	storm	blow	feel	soft
wind	fast	strong	outside	power

1.	2.
3.	4.

Keeping Score
If the guessers answer correctly, they get 1 point.
The first pair to get 3 points wins!

Reread and Explain: Cause-and-Effect Chart

I Face the Wind

Explain the effects of the wind in the story. Use the Cause-and-Effect Chart.

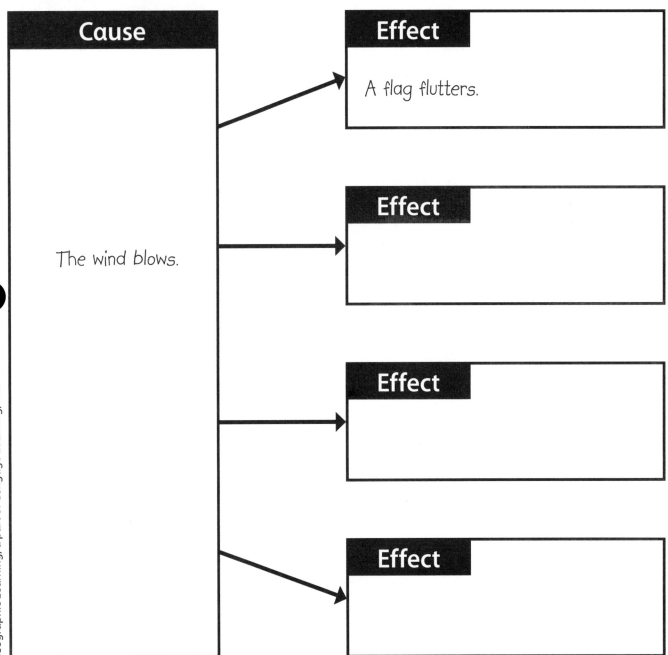

Cause	Effect
The wind blows.	A flag flutters.
	Effect
	Effect
	Effect

Tell a partner facts you learned about the wind in "I Face the Wind." Use your Cause-and-Effect Chart.

National Geographic Learning, a part of Cengage Learning, Inc.

Name _____   Date _____

I Face the Wind

Use this passage to practice reading with proper expression.

1 Open a large plastic bag.   6

    Make sure there are no holes in it.   14

2 Pull the bag through the air so it puffs up.   25

3 Twist it closed to trap the air you caught.   35

4 Squeeze the bag to feel the air.   43

Expression

B ☐ Does not read with feeling.	A ☐ Reads with appropriate feeling for most content.
I ☐ Reads with some feeling, but does not match content.	AH ☐ Reads with appropriate feeling for all content.

Accuracy and Rate Formula

Use the formula to measure a reader's accuracy and rate while reading aloud.

$$\frac{\rule{3cm}{0.4pt}}{\substack{\text{words attempted} \\ \text{in one minute}}} - \frac{\rule{3cm}{0.4pt}}{\text{number of errors}} = \frac{\rule{3cm}{0.4pt}}{\substack{\text{words correct per} \\ \text{minute (wcpm)}}}$$

National Geographic Learning, a part of Cengage Learning, Inc.

Respond and Extend: Two-Column Chart

Character's Actions

Read Gluscabi's actions. Write the reason for his actions in the chart.

Gluscabi's Actions	Reasons
Gluscabi went to see Wind Eagle.	There was too much wind. Gluscabi couldn't fish.
Gluscabi put Wind Eagle in a hole.	
Gluscabi went to see Wind Eagle again.	
Gluscabi took Wind Eagle out of the hole.	

Choose one of Gluscabi's actions. With a partner, share Gluscabi's reason.

Grammar: Sentence Types

Outside

Grammar Rules Sentence Types

1. A statement tells something.
2. A question asks something.
3. An exclamation shows strong feeling.
4. A command tells someone to do something.

You can play outside in the park today. Work with a partner to write about it.

1. Write a statement that tells what you can do in the park.

   I can ride my bike.

2. Write a question about the park.

   _____

3. Tell your friend to bring something to the park.

   _____

4. Write to show how you feel about playing in the park.

   _____

Classify Details

Classify activities people do in different kinds of weather.

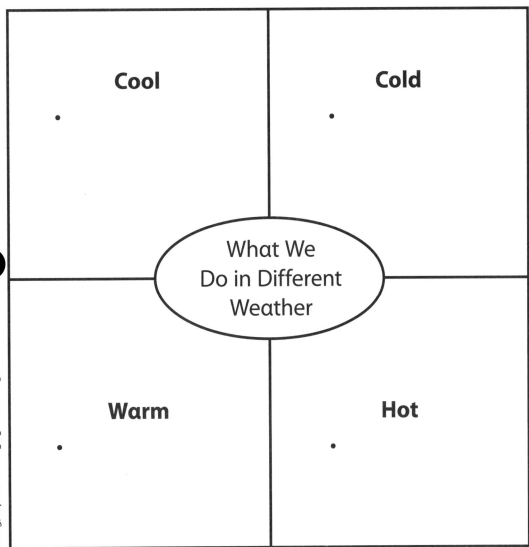

Grammar: Yes/No Questions

Make a Match

Grammar Rules Yes/No Questions

Yes/No questions begin with a verb.

- Answer with *yes* or *no*.
- Use the same verb in the answer.

Is it cloudy?

Yes, it is cloudy.

1. Partner 1 points to a Question Card.

2. Partner 2 points to an Answer Card.

3. If the question and the answer match, cross out both cards.

4. Play until all the cards are crossed out.

Question Cards	
Is it snowing?	Is it windy?
Is it sunny?	Is it raining?

Answer Cards	
No, it is not windy.	Yes, it is raining.
Yes, it is sunny.	No, it is not snowing.

 Ask the questions. Have your partner answer. Take turns.

Key Points Reading

A Year for Kiko

January
Snow is falling on Kiko.

February
Kiko's window is cold and white.

March
Wind blows Kiko's hair.

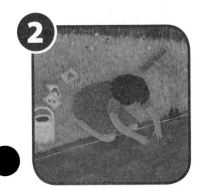

April
Rain falls on the earth.

May
Kiko plants a seed.

June
Kiko picks strawberries.

July
Kiko chases fireflies.

August
It is hot. Kiko swims to get cool.

September
Crickets sing.

October
Red and gold leaves are falling.

November
Kiko looks for the moon.

December
Kiko wears her coat, mittens, and hat.

Who? What? Where?

Grammar Rules Question Words

Start a question with a question word.

who, what, where, when, why, how

Complete the questions. Use *how, who, when, where,* or *why.*

1. _____ Who _____ has an umbrella?

2. _____ can we build a snowman?

3. _____ is my hat?

4. _____ cold is it outside?

5. _____ is it so hot?

Write a new question using one of the question words. Ask a partner your question.

● **Vocabulary: Apply Word Knowledge**

Rivet

1. Write the first letter of each word.
2. Try to guess the word.
3. Fill in the other letters of the word.

1. __ __ __ __

2. __ __ __ __

3. __ __ __

4. _____

● 5. __ __ __ __ __

6. __ __ __ __ __

7. __ __ __ __ __ __ __

8. __ __ __ __

9. __ __ __ __

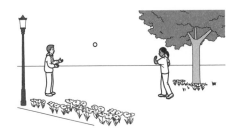

10. __ __ __ __ __

11. __ __ __ __

12. __ __ __ __

 Take turns with a partner. Choose a word. Say it in a sentence.

A Year for Kiko

Add details to the Classification Chart about things Kiko does in different weather.

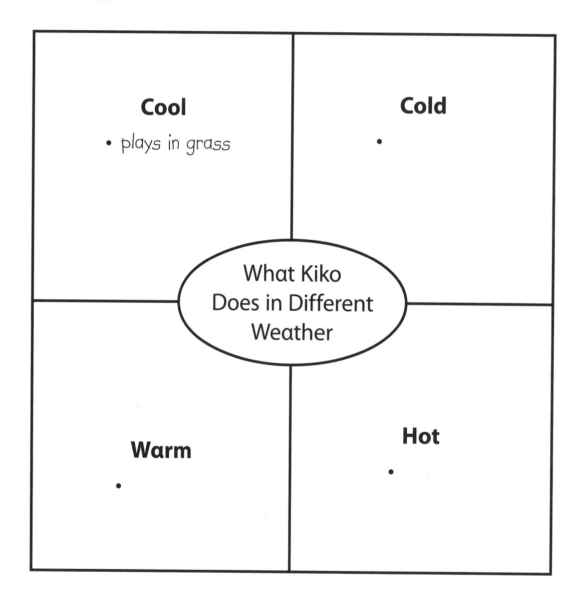

Cool
• plays in grass

Cold
•

What Kiko Does in Different Weather

Warm
•

Hot
•

 Retell "A Year for Kiko" to a partner. Use your chart and illustrations in the story.

A Year for Kiko

Use this passage to practice reading with proper expression.

In December Kiko breathes out 5

clouds. She puts on her winter coat. 12

She wears her mittens and hat. 18

Kiko is ready for snow. 23

Expression

| B | ☐ Does not read with feeling. | | A | ☐ Reads with appropriate feeling for most content. |

| I | ☐ Reads with some feeling, but does not match content. | | AH | ☐ Reads with appropriate feeling for all content. |

Accuracy and Rate Formula

Use the formula to measure a reader's accuracy and rate while reading aloud.

_____ − _____ = _____
words attempted   number of errors   words correct per
in one minute   minute (wcpm)

Respond and Extend: T Chart

Compare Genres

Compare a story and an interview.

Realistic Fiction	Interview
has characters	has real people

 Use your T chart to talk about which kind of text you like best. Give reasons.

National Geographic Learning, a part of Cengage Learning, Inc.

Who? What? Where?

Grammar Rules Ask Questions

Question Words	Information
Who	person
Where	place
What	thing or action
Why	reason
When	time
How	way something is done

Circle the question word. Then write the type of information it gives. Choose from *person, place, thing, reason, time,* **or** *way something is done.*

1. (When) are we going ice skating?  _time_

2. Where is the park? - - - - - - - - - - -

3. What should I bring? - - - - - - - - -

4. Who is going? - - - - - - - - - -

Write a new question about the park. Use a question word. Have a partner say the type of information it gives.

Writing Project: Rubric

Ideas

	Is the message clear and focused?	Do the details show the writer knows the topic?
4	❑ All of the writing is clear and focused.	❑ All the details tell about the topic. The writer knows the topic well.
3	❑ Most of the writing is clear and focused.	❑ Most of the details are about the topic. The writer knows the topic fairly well.
2	❑ Some of the writing is not clear. The writing lacks some focus.	❑ Some details are about the topic. The writer doesn't know the topic well.
1	❑ The writing is not clear or focused.	❑ Many details are not about the topic. The writer does not know the topic.

Writing Project: Prewrite

Weather Cause-and-Effects Chart

Write one kind of weather in the left box under **Cause**. Write four things that can happen during that type of weather in the right box under **Effects**.

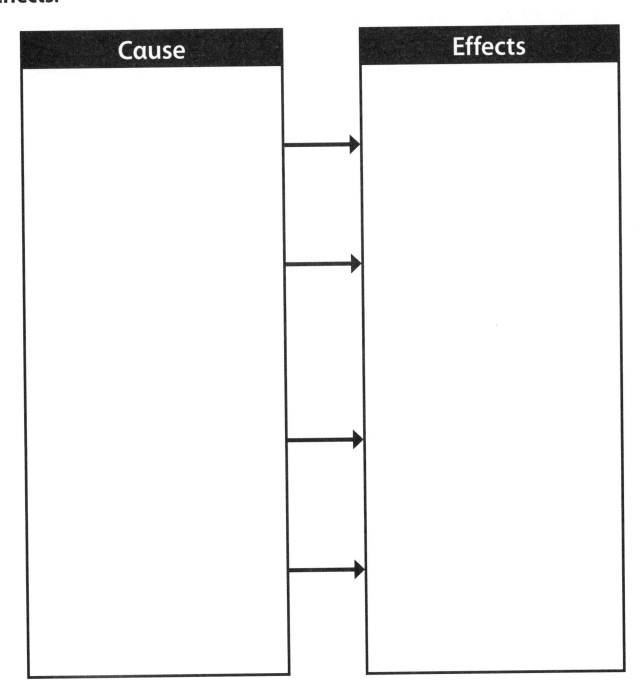

Writing Project

Revise

Use the Revising Marks to revise this paragraph. Look for:

- examples to explain the idea windy weather
- vivid or interesting words

Revising Marks	
^	Add.
℘	Take out.
⬭⤴	Move to here.

Kites are in the air. Trees bend. These things all happen because

the weather is windy. Leaves fall. The wind goes over the hills.

Name _____   Date _____

Edit and Proofread

Use the Revising Marks to edit and proofread this paragraph. Look for:

- **correct spelling of vowel digraphs**
- **missing letters**
- **correct end marks**

Editing Marks	
∧	Add.
⅋	Take out.
⬯⌒	Move to here.
⬯	Check spelling.
≡	Capitalize.
⊙	Add a period.
?	Add a question mark.
!	Add an exclamation point.

kites dance in the air. Trees bend and sway? Do you hear the

leaves. Whoosh! This all happens because the weather is winddy.

The wind blos over the hills.

National Geographic Learning, a part of Cengage Learning, Inc.

Unit Concept Map

Then and Now

Make a concept map with the answers to the Big Question: What's the difference between then and now?

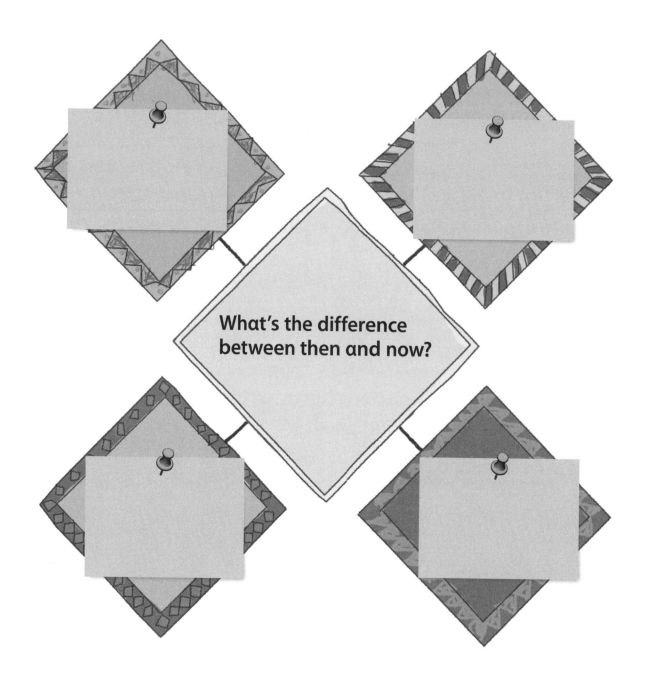

What's the difference between then and now?

Identify Main Idea and Details

Complete the diagram. Write different ways people communicate.

People communicate in different ways.

National Geographic Learning, a part of Cengage Learning, Inc.

Name _____   Date _____

What Happened Yesterday?

Grammar Rules Regular Past Tense

Add -*ed* to many action verbs to show that action happened in the past.

verb + -*ed* = past tense

call + -*ed* = called

Yesterday I <u>called</u> my aunt.

Read each sentence. Add -ed to each bolded word. Write the new word.

1. I _____ mailed _____ a letter. **mail**

2. You _____ me on your cell phone. **call**

3. She _____ the news on TV. **watch**

4. We _____ a game on the computer. **play**

5. They _____ to the radio. **listen**

 Tell a partner about one thing you did yesterday.

Communication Then and Now

1 Communication is sharing news and ideas. Talking, writing, and body language are all ways to communicate. Communication is now better and faster than in the past.

2 In the past, people copied each book by hand. Now books are printed on machines. You can read books on computers, too.

3 In the past, people sent messages with telegraph machines. Now people call each other on telephones. People also wrote letters in the past. Now people send e-mail messages on computers.

4 In the past, people bought newspapers to read. Now people have newspapers delivered. They also read them on the internet. Communication will continue to change. What will happen next?

Grammar: Irregular Past Tense

That Was Then

Grammar Rules Irregular Past Tense

Some verbs change a lot to tell about the past.

Present	Past
am, is	was
are	were
go	went
do	did

Read each sentence. Circle the correct form of the verb in ( ).

1. My aunt (do, (did)) her homework on paper.

2. Today I (do, did) my homework on the computer.

3. Long ago, people (go, went) by horse.

4. Now, people (go, went) by car.

5. Then, the news (is, was) on the radio.

6. Today, the news (is, was) on the Internet.

 Say a sentence using *was*, *were*, *did*, or *went* to a partner.

© National Geographic Learning, a part of Cengage Learning, Inc.

Around the World

1. **The traveler stands behind a challenger.**

2. **Listen to the clue. Find the Key Word and say it.**

3. **The first to answer correctly travels to the next student on the right. The first traveler to go all around the circle wins.**

news	computer	message	past	future

CLUES

- We can send a _____ with e-mail.

- I have some _____ to share with you about our school.

- In the _____, I will be an adult.

- My mom reads e-books on her _____.

- In the _____, I was a baby.

Communication Then and Now

Complete the diagram below. Write about how communication has changed.

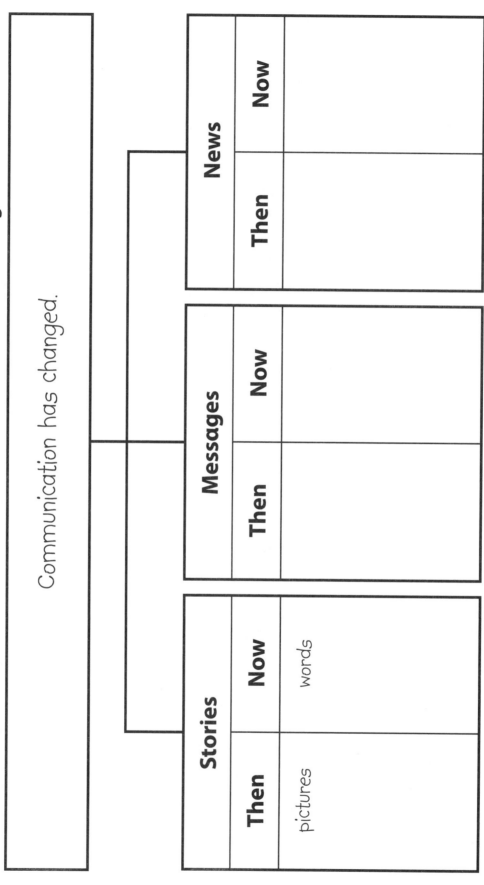

Communication has changed.

Stories

Then	Now
pictures	words

Messages

Then	Now

News

Then	Now

Use your diagram to retell the article to a partner.

Fluency: Intonation

Communication Then and Now

Use the passage to practice reading with proper intonation.

Long ago, people copied each book. If   7

they wanted 10 copies of a book, they had   16

to write out each copy one at a time.   25

Now, machines make printed   29

books or e-books. Printed books   34

are made with printing presses. People   40

read e-books on computers.   44

Intonation

| B | ☐ Does not change pitch. | A | ☐ Changes pitch to match some of the content. |
| I | ☐ Changes pitch, but does not match content. | AH | ☐ Changes pitch to match all content. |

Accuracy and Rate Formula

Use the formula to measure a reader's accuracy and rate while reading aloud.

$$\underline{\hspace{3cm}} - \underline{\hspace{3cm}} = \underline{\hspace{3cm}}$$

words attempted   number of errors   words correct per
in one minute   minute (wcpm)

Compare Genres

Compare a history article and a blog entry.

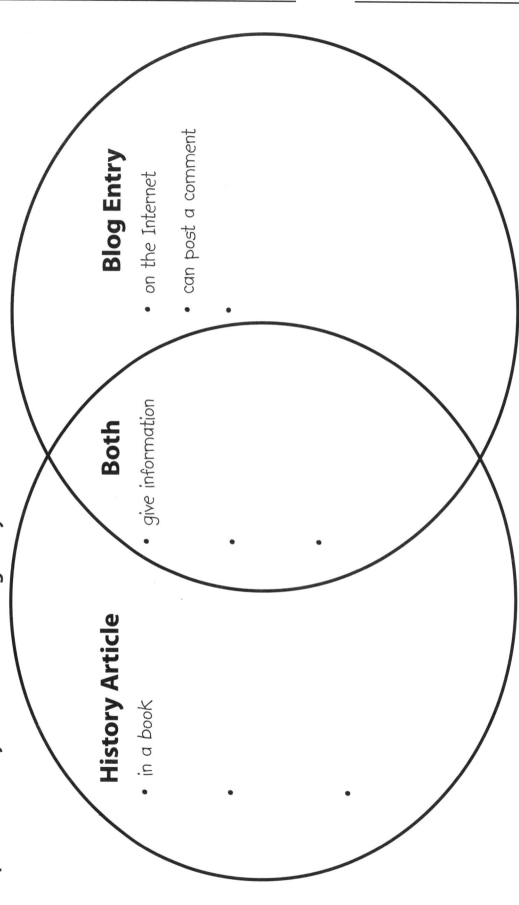

Blog Entry

- on the Internet
- can post a comment
-

Both

- give information
-
-

History Article

- in a book
-
-

Take turns with a partner. Express your opinion about a history article and a blog entry.

Name _____   Date _____

Make It Past Tense

Grammar Rules Past Tense Verbs

To make a verb about the past:

- Add -ed to the end of a regular verb, like *watch*.
- Use a special form of the an irregular verb, like *fly*.

1. **Play with a partner.**
2. **Spin the spinner.**
3. **Change the verb to the past tense.**

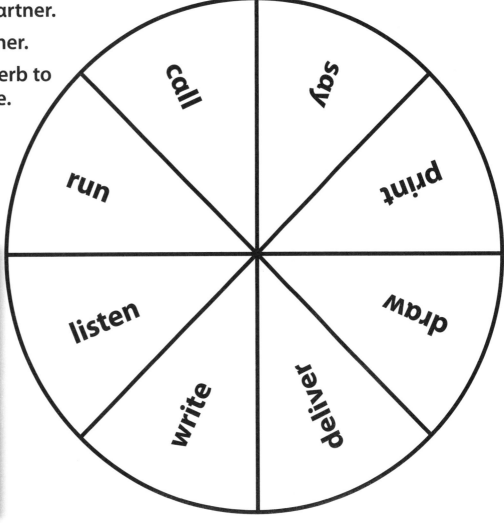

Make a Spinner

1. Put a paper clip ⬭ in the center of the circle.

2. Hold one end of the paper clip with a pencil.

3. Spin the paper clip around the pencil.

Thinking Map: Character Description Chart

Describe Character's Feelings

List what Marta's mother says or does. Then describe what this shows about how she feels.

Character	What the Character Says or Does	What This Shows About How the Character Feels
Marta's mother		

7.11

Grammar: Future Tense with *will*

When?

Grammar Rules Future Tense with *will*

Add *will* in front of a verb to make it future tense.

I <u>will</u> call my friend on the phone.

Read each sentence. Use the correct tense of the bold word to complete the sentence.

1. We _____ will visit _____ our family next week. **visit**

2. They _____ us at the airport yesterday. **meet**

3. We _____ at their house tomorrow. **stay**

4. We _____ to the zoo soon. **go**

5. Last night we _____ a movie. **watch**

6. We _____ ice cream after dinner. **eat**

Tell a partner what you will do after school today.

Key Points Reading

A New Old Tune

1

Max helps Aunt Nell get ready for a yard sale. He finds a large disk. Aunt Nell explains that it is a record. She shows him how it plays on a record player.

2

Aunt Nell says that things change. She had a black and white TV. She had a phone with a cord.

3

Aunt Nell says that some new things are easier to use. But some things stay the same. People still like to talk on the phone. They like to watch TV, listen to music, and dance.

National Geographic Learning, a part of Cengage Learning, Inc.

Grammar: Future Tense with *am/is/are going to*

Let's Go!

Grammar Rules Future Tense with *am/is/are going to*

To make verbs about the future, add these words before the verb:

Future	Example
am going to	I <u>am going</u> to build a house.
is going to	He <u>is going</u> to make a cake.
are going to	You <u>are going</u> to invent a machine.

Complete the sentences. Write *am going to*, *is going to*, or *are going to*.

1. Junko <u>is going to</u> play soccer.

2. Aunt Lin and Mom _____ take a walk.

3. I _____ jump rope.

4. He _____ run a race.

5. You _____ skate.

💬 **With a partner, write sentences about recess. Use *am going to*, *is going to*, and *are going to*.**

National Geographic Learning, a part of Cengage Learning, Inc.

Vocabulary: Apply Word Knowledge

Picture It

1. Form pairs. Choose a pair to be the artists and a pair to be the guessers.

2. The artists secretly select a Key Word.

3. The artists draw a picture to show the word's meaning.

4. The guessers guess what Key Word the picture shows.

5. Switch roles.

record	music	better	tool	easier	new
old	invent	machine	build	modern	feel

1.	2.
3.	4.

Keeping Score

If the guessers answer correctly, they get 1 point.
The first pair to get 3 points wins!

● **Reread and Retell: Character Description Chart**

A New Old Tune

List the things Max and Nell say or do. Then describe what this shows about how the character feels.

Character	What the Character Says or Does	What This Shows About How the Character Feels
Max	• Wow •	• He feels surprised. •
Nell	• •	• •

💬 **Use your chart to retell the story to a partner.**

Fluency: Expression

A New Old Tune

Use the passage to practice reading with proper expression.

"Has anything stayed the same?"   5

asked Max.   7

"Yes," said Aunt Nell. "People still   13

love to talk on the telephone. And watch   21

television. And listen to music."   26

"And dance!" added Max.   30

Expression

B ☐ Does not read with feeling.   A ☐ Reads with appropriate feeling for most content.

I ☐ Reads with some feeling, but does not match content.   AH ☐ Reads with appropriate feeling for all content.

Accuracy and Rate Formula

Use the formula to measure a reader's accuracy and rate while reading aloud.

$$\underline{\qquad\qquad} - \underline{\qquad\qquad} = \underline{\qquad\qquad}$$

| words attempted in one minute | number of errors | words correct per minute (wcpm) |

National Geographic Learning, a part of Cengage Learning, Inc.

Respond and Extend: Venn Diagram

Compare Genres

Compare a story and poetry.

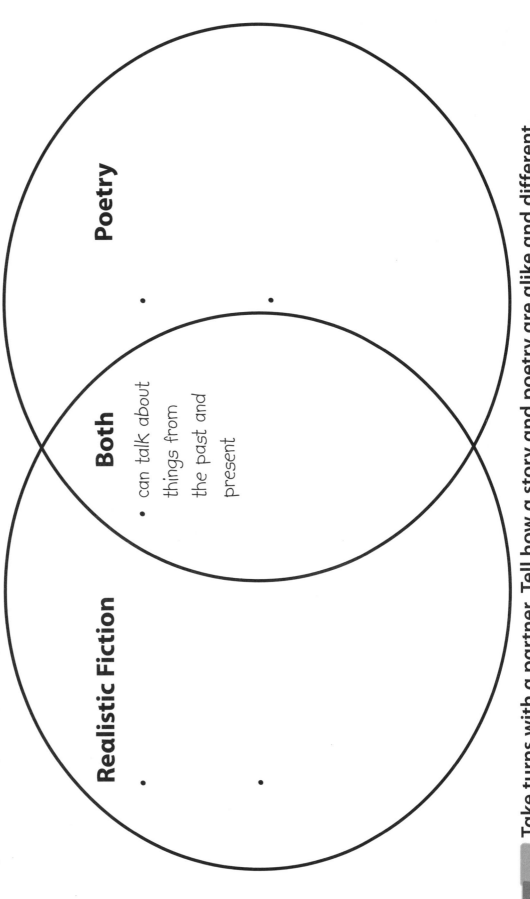

Poetry

Both
- can talk about things from the past and present

Realistic Fiction

Take turns with a partner. Tell how a story and poetry are alike and different.

Grammar: Future Tense Verbs

Make It Happen

Grammar Rules Future Tense Verbs

To make verbs about the future, add *will, am going to, is going to,* or *are going to* before the verb.

You <u>will</u> listen to music. He <u>is going to</u> read a book.

1. **Play with a partner.**

2. **Choose one word from the Future and Verb columns below. Create as many sentences as you can.**

3. **Cross out the words you choose.**

4. **Your partner takes a turn.**

5. **The player who writes the most complete sentences wins.**

Future	Verb
will	build
am going to	invent
is going to	make
are going to	write
will	draw

onal Geographic Learning, a part of Cengage Learning, Inc.

Writing Project: Rubric

Organization

	Is the writing well-organized? Does it fit the writer's purpose?	Does the writing flow?
4	❑ The writing is very well-organized. ❑ It clearly fits the writer's purpose.	❑ The writing is smooth and logical. Each sentence flows into the next one.
3	❑ Most of the writing is organized. ❑ It mostly fits the writer's purpose.	❑ Most of the writing is smooth. There are only a few sentences that do not flow logically.
2	❑ The writing is not well-organized. ❑ It fits the writer's purpose somewhat.	❑ Some of the writing is smooth. Many sentences do not flow smoothly.
1	❑ The writing is not organized at all. ❑ It does not fit the writer's purpose.	❑ The sentences do not flow smoothly or logically.

Writing Project: Prewrite

Main Idea and Details Diagram

Write the old object you chose in the Main Idea box at the top. Write descriptions in the smaller Detail boxes.

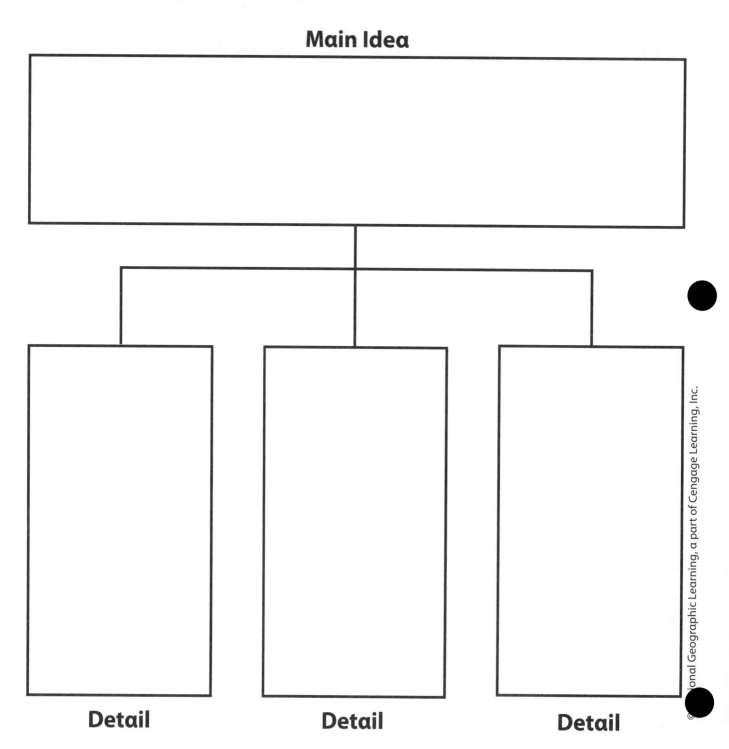

Main Idea

Detail   **Detail**   **Detail**

Writing Project

Revise

Use the Revising Marks to revise this friendly letter. Look for:

- **parts of the letter**
- **specific words**

Revising Marks	
∧	Add.
℘	Take out.
⌒⌐	Move to here.

January 10

Dear Maria,

my grandpa took me to a show. One car was older

than him! That old car had skinny wheels. It did not have

seatbelts. I think that old car is not safe.

Marta

Name _____ Date _____

Edit and Proofread

Use the Editing Marks to edit and
proofread this friendly letter. Look for:

- correct spelling of silent consonants
- words that sound alike
- correct use of past and
  future verbs
- a capital letters on names
  and months

Editing Marks	
∧	Add.
ℐ	Take out.
⬯	Check spelling.
≡	Capitalize.

january 10

Dear maria,

Grandma Rose take me to a store last week. It had a sine that said

"Out of the Past." We saw an old ink pen that people used to rite in

school. They called it a fountain pen. You have to put the ink in it. She

said she had one at school when she was little. I think it must have

been very messy. She said she show me how to use one next week.

Your friend,

Marta

Unit Concept Map

Get out the Map!

Make a concept map with the answers to the Big Question: Why do we need maps?

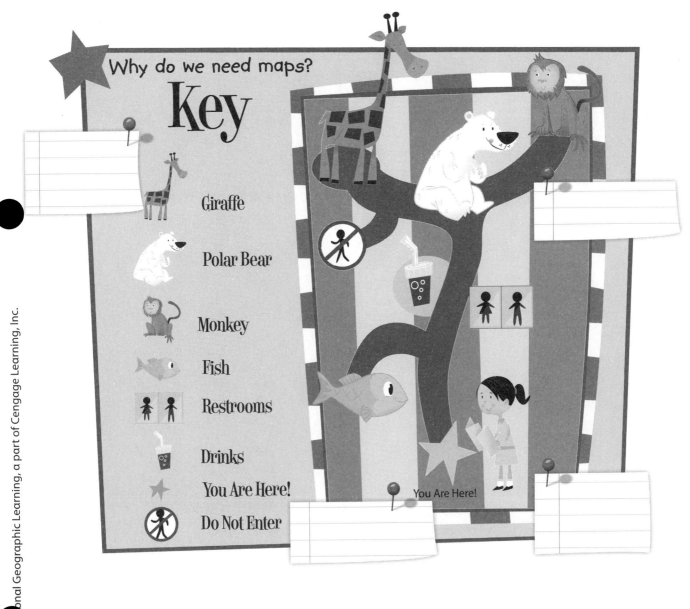

Thinking Map: T Chart

Use Information

Draw symbols and signs that you see in town. Then write what they mean in the column on the right.

Symbols and Signs	What It Means

Find the Adverb!

Grammar Rules Adverbs that Tell How

1. An adverb can tell how something happens.
2. These adverbs end in *-ly*.

   She spoke slowly.

Underline the verb in each sentence. Circle the adverb.

1. Jim <u>looked</u> (carefully) at the map.

2. Lisa asked loudly for directions.

3. She kindly gave her directions.

4. We were finally on our way.

5. We turned quickly around the corner.

6. My mom drove slowly in front of my friend's house.

 Work with a partner. Put adverb word cards in a paper bag. Take turns to act it out and say it in a sentence.

National Geographic Learning, a part of Cengage Learning, Inc.

Name _____   Date _____

If Maps Could Talk

1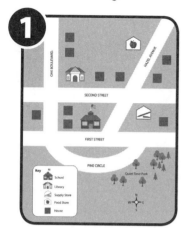

Maps use symbols to show where things are. Read the key to learn the meanings of map symbols.

2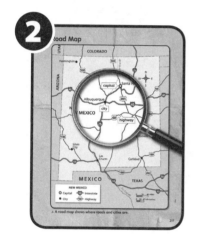

Symbols on a road map help drivers find their way. Symbols on a weather map show what the weather will be.

3

Some maps don't have keys. These maps use picture symbols of real things.

Grammar: Adverbs that Tell Where, When

Where? When?

Grammar Rules Adverbs that Tell Where, When

1. Some adverbs tell where something happens. *We turned <u>left</u>.*
2. Some adverbs tell when something happens. *We will arrive <u>tomorrow</u>.*

1. Toss a marker onto one of the adverbs below.
2. Use the adverb in a sentence. Create as many sentences as you can.
3. Your partner takes a turn.
4. The player who writes the most correct sentences wins.

there	later
today	nearby
yesterday	away
everywhere	first
next	here

 Take turns with a partner. Read aloud two of your sentences.

8.5

Around the World

1. The traveler stands behind a challenger.

2. Listen to the clue. Find the Key Word and say it.

3. The first to answer correctly travels to the next student on the right. The first traveler to go all around the circle wins.

Symbol!

map	key	meaning	symbol	picture	useful

CLUES

- A _____ can be a shape or picture.

- A _____ tells the meaning of a map's symbols.

- A map is _____ for finding places.

- He drew a _____ of a house.

- Look on the _____ to find the library.

- A key shows the _____ of a symbol or sign.

Name _____   Date _____

If Maps Could Talk

Draw symbols and signs from "If Maps Could Talk." Write their meanings in the column on the right.

Symbols and Signs	What It Means
	• mostly sunny
	•
	•

 Take turns with a partner. Tell what you learned about signs, symbols, and maps from the text.

Name _____ Date _____

Fluency: Phrasing

If Maps Could Talk

Use this passage to practice reading with proper phrasing.

Step 1

Draw the outline of your school. Show what   2
                                                     10
your school would look like from above.   17

Step 2
                                                     19
Draw your classroom as a square.   25

Put a symbol in the classroom,   31

such as a star.   35

Step 3
                                                     37
Draw other rooms in your school,   43

like the cafeteria. Add hallways,   48

restrooms, and doors.   51

Phrasing

B ☐ Rarely pauses while reading text.   A ☐ Frequently pauses at appropriate points in the text.

I ☐ Occasionally pauses while reading text.   AH ☐ Consistently pauses at all appropriate points in the text.

Accuracy and Rate Formula

Use the formula to measure a reader's accuracy and rate while reading aloud.

$$\frac{\qquad}{\substack{\text{words attempted} \\ \text{in one minute}}} - \frac{\qquad}{\text{number of errors}} = \frac{\qquad}{\substack{\text{words correct per} \\ \text{minute (wcpm)}}}$$

National Geographic Learning, a part of Cengage Learning, Inc.

Respond and Extend: T Chart

Compare Genres

Compare an informational text and a poem.

Informational Text	Poem
gives definitions	uses words to create images in your mind

Take turns with a partner. Ask questions about an informational text and a poem.

National Geographic Learning, a part of Cengage Learning, Inc.

Name _____ Date _____

Trip to the Train Station

Grammar Rules Adverbs

Adverbs can tell:

- **how** something happens.
- **where** something happens.
- **when** something happens.

Read the passage. Categorize the underlined adverbs in the chart below.

My grandfather and I walked <u>quickly</u> to the train station. We turned <u>left</u> at the corner. Then we turned <u>right</u> on Park Street. We waited <u>patiently</u> for the train. The train will arrive <u>soon</u>.

Adverbs		
Where	**How** quickly	**When**
_____	_____	_____
_____	_____	_____
_____	_____	_____

 With a partner, add more adverbs to the chart. Use one of the adverbs in a sentence.

Name _____ Date _____

Identify Problem and Solution

Tell a different story about Jack. Imagine Jack is with a friend. Complete the Problem-and-Solution Chart.

Problem:

↓

Event 1:
Event 2:

↓

Solution:

National Geographic Learning, a part of Cengage Learning, Inc.

Grammar: Prepositions Tell Where, Show Direction

Where Is It?

Grammar Rules Prepositions Tell Where, Show Direction

1. Prepositions can tell where things are.

My house is <u>next to</u> a park.

2. Prepositions can tell a direction, or a way to go.

My mom and I walk <u>to</u> the park.

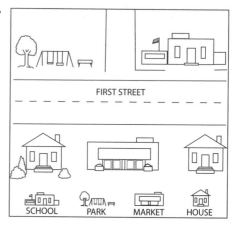

FIRST STREET

SCHOOL   PARK   MARKET   HOUSE

Read each sentence. Look at the map. Circle the correct word. Write the word.

1. A school is ----- **on** ----- First Street.   in

2. A market is ------------------------ the houses.   inside   between

3. A house is ------------------------ from the school.   around   across

4. A park is ------------------------ the school.   next to   into

Look at the map. Write a new sentence using a preposition.
Read it to a partner.

Key Points Reading

Caperucita Roja

Caperucita Roja lived in a village south of a forest. Her Abuelita was sick. Caperucita Roja went to visit her. She took a map to help her.

Caperucita Roja followed her map. Suddenly, Big Bad Wolf came out of the forest. He wanted to eat Caperucita Roja. Too many people were watching. Then he had an idea.

The wolf looked at his map. He found a different way to Abuelita's house. He put Abuelita in the closet. He put on her nightgown. He pretended that he was Abuelita. He was going to eat Caperucita Roja!

Caperucita Roja got to Abuelita's house. She looked inside. She saw two long ears, a very long nose, and two black eyes. That wasn't Abuelita! She went to the farmer's house. She asked for help. The wolf saw the farmer. He jumped out of the window and ran away.

Name _____   Date _____

On My Desk

Grammar Rules Prepositional Phrases

A prepositional phrase is a small group of words.

- Begin a prepositional phrase with a preposition.

  The teacher walks (around) the desk.

Read the sentence. Circle the preposition. Underline the prepositional phrase.

1. I walk (to) my desk.

2. There is a book on my desk.

3. My bag is next to my chair.

4. A pencil fell under my desk.

5. I walk out of the classroom.

💬 Write a sentence with a prepositional phrase. Read your sentence to a partner. Ask your partner to say the prepositional phrase.

Name _____ Date _____

Picture It

1. **Form pairs. Choose a pair to be the artists and a pair to be the guessers.**

2. **The artists secretly select a Key Word.**

3. **The artists draw a picture to show the word's meaning**

4. **The guessers guess what Key Word the picture shows.**

5. **Switch roles.**

path	north	south	east	west	near
left	right	location	direction	far	follow

1.	2.
3.	4.

Keeping Score

If the guessers answer correctly, they get 1 point.

The first pair to get 3 points wins!

Name _____ Date _____

Caperucita Roja

List the events and solution to the problem below.

Problem: Big Bad Wolf is trying to eat Abuelita.

Event 1:

Event 2:

Event 3:

Solution:

 Use your Problem-and-Solution Chart to retell the story to a partner.

© National Geographic Learning, a part of Cengage Learning, Inc.

Fluency: Expression

Caperucita Roja

Use this passage to practice reading with proper expression.

One day, Caperucita Roja's Mamá said,   6

"Hija, Abuelita is sick. Take her some food.   14

Visit with her for a while."   20

"Sí, Mamá," Caperucita Roja said.   25

"I will go now."   29

"Follow the shortest path. Do not get   36

distracted. Go quickly!" Mamá said.   41

"Do not forget your map."   46

"Sí, Mamá. I will take the map with   54

me," said Caperucita Roja.   58

Expression

B ☐ Does not read with feeling.	A ☐ Reads with appropriate feeling for most content.
I ☐ Reads with some feeling, but does not match content.	AH ☐ Reads with appropriate feeling for all content.

Accuracy and Rate Formula

Use the formula to measure a reader's accuracy and rate while reading aloud.

_____ − _____ = _____
words attempted   number of errors   words correct per minute
in one minute   (wcpm)

Compare Genres

Compare a fairy tale and a how-to article.

Fairy Tale	How-to Article
tells a story that cannot happen in real life	tells how to make something that is real

💬 **Take turns with a partner. Tell how a fairy tale and a how-to article are different.**

Name _____ Date _____

Grammar: Prepositions

The Preposition Game

Grammar Rules Prepositions

Prepositions can tell where. Put prepositions before a noun that names a place.	The book is <u>on</u> the <u>table</u>.

next to	across	between	under
at			**down**
BEGIN			**in**
			over
END			
into	on	above	up

1. Play with a partner.
2. Use a small object for a game piece.
3. Flip a coin.

   (coin) = Move 1 space.

   (coin) = Move 2 spaces.

4. Use the preposition in a sentence.
5. Write the prepositional phrase on another sheet of paper.
6. The first one to the END wins!

Name _____   Date _____

Caperucita Roja Saves Abuelita

Setting: The play takes place inside Abuelita's house and in the farmer's field.

Cast of Characters: Narrator, Caperucita Roja, Big Bad Wolf, Farmer, Abuelita

Scene 1: At Abuelita's house

Caperucita Roja is standing inside the bedroom door at Abuelita's house. Big Bad Wolf is in Abuelita's bed, wearing her nightgown and nightcap. The blankets are pulled up under his chin, and he is trying to make himself look smaller. Caperucita Roja is looking at him suspiciously.

Narrator: Caperucita Roja's Abuelita doesn't feel well. Caperucita Roja wants to visit Abuelita. When she gets to Abuelita's house, something is wrong.

Caperucita Roja: Hola, Abuelita! How are you today?

Big Bad Wolf makes himself smaller and pulls the blankets up even higher.

Big Bad Wolf: Oh, I am fine! Come closer, Caperucita Roja. I want to eat … I mean, I want to see you!

Caperucita Roja takes a small step toward Big Bad Wolf.

Caperucita Roja: But, Abuelita, those are not your ears. That is not your nose. And those are not your eyes! You are not Abuelita! You are Big Bad Wolf!

Caperucita Roja runs out of the house. She is frightened.

Narrator: Caperucita Roja thinks. She wants to save Abuelita. She needs help.

Caperucita Roja: Who can help me? The farmer can!

Caperucita Roja pulls out her map. She looks at it quickly and carefully.

Caperucita Roja: I will run east. I will find the farmer. He will help me.

Caperucita Roja runs offstage.

Scene 2: In the farmer's field

Caperucita Roja is talking to the farmer. They are standing in a field with a few piles of hay. A scarecrow is behind them.

Narrator: Caperucita Roja finds the farmer in his field. She tells him Big Bad Wolf is at Abuelita's house.

Farmer: I scare the rabbits in my field. I will scare Big Bad Wolf. I will save Abuelita!

Caperucita Roja: Come on! Let's go!

Caperucita Roja and the farmer run offstage.

Scene 3: At Abuelita's house

The farmer runs through the door of Abuelita's room. Caperucita Roja is behind him. Big Bad Wolf jumps out of bed. He looks very frightened.

Narrator: When Big Bad Wolf sees the farmer, he is scared. He tries to get away, but the farmer is fast. Big Bad Wolf jumps out of the window. He runs into the forest.

Big Bad Wolf jumps out of a window. He runs offstage. Caperucita Roja opens the closet door. Abuelita steps out. Caperucita Roja helps her get into bed.

Caperucita Roja: Oh, Abuelita! You are safe! I am so happy.

Abuelita: Thank you, Caperucita Roja! You are a good girl!

Caperucita Roja: And thank you, Farmer!

Farmer: You are welcome, Caperucita Roja. I am happy Abuelita is safe!

Narrator: Now Abuelita and the farmer are friends. They never see Big Bad Wolf again. And Caperucita Roja visits Abuelita often. They are all very happy.

End of play

Writing Project: Rubric

Ideas

	Is the message clear and focused?	Do the details show the writer knows the topic?
4	❑ All of the writing is clear and focused.	❑ All the details tell about the topic. The writer knows the topic well.
3	❑ Most of the writing is clear and focused.	❑ Most of the details are about the topic. The writer knows the topic fairly well.
2	❑ Some of the writing is not clear. The writing lacks some focus.	❑ Some details are about the topic. The writer doesn't know the topic well.
1	❑ The writing is not clear or focused.	❑ Many details are not about the topic. The writer does not know the topic.

Writing Project: Prewrite

Problem-and-Solution Chart

Write the story problem in the top box. Write the events that happen in the middle boxes. Write the solution in the bottom box.

Problem:

Event 1:

Event 2:

Solution:

Name _____ Date _____

Revise

Use the Revising Marks to revise this
paragraph. Look for:

- a story title
- a problem
- a solution
- an opinion about the story
- varied sentences

Revising Marks	
∧	Add.
℘	Take out.
⬯⌐	Move to here.

I read "A New Old Tune" by Pat Cummings. Max helps his Aunt

Nell get ready for a yard sale. He finds some some old things. One

thing he finds is a record. Max doesn't know what it is or how to

play it. Aunt Nell and Max dance I like this story

Writing Project

Edit and Proofread

Use the Editing Marks to edit and proofread this literary response. Look for:

- **correct spelling of prefixes and suffixes**
- **capital letters at beginning of sentences**
- **correct adverbs and prepositions**

Editing Marks	
∧	Add.
⌐	Take out.
⬭	Check spelling.
≡	Capitalize.

The Three Little Pigs

by Pin-mei Yau

I read The "Three Little Pigs." a big, bad wolf wanted to eat the three little pigs.

The pigs quickle built three houses. The wolf blew down the unnsafe houses of straw and sticks. the wolf could not blow the brick house down, and he left in a quickly.

The three little pigs were safe of the brick house. i think the wolf leaving made "The Three Little Pigs" a good story.

Acknowledgments

Grateful acknowledgment is given to the authors, artists, photographers, museums, publishers, and agents for permission to reprint copyrighted material. Every effort has been made to secure the appropriate permission. If any omissions have been made or if corrections are required, please contact the Publisher.

Cover Illustration: Joel Sotelo

Please see the Level B Reach Student Book for all image acknowledgments.

For product information and technology assistance, contact us at
Customer & Sales Support, 888-915-3276

For permission to use material from this text or product, submit all requests online at **www.cengage.com/permissions**
Further permissions questions can be emailed to
permissionrequest@cengage.com

National Geographic Learning | Cengage Learning
1 Lower Ragsdale Drive
Building 1, Suite 200
Monterey, CA 93940

Cengage Learning is a leading provider of customized learning solutions with office locations around the globe, including Singapore, the United Kingdom, Australia, Mexico, Brazil, and Japan. Locate your local office at **www.cengage.com/global**.

Visit National Geographic Learning online at **NGL.Cengage.com**
Visit our corporate website at **www.cengage.com**

ISBN: 978-1-3371-0989-5 (Practice Book)

ISBN: 978-1-3371-0995-6 (Practice Masters)
Teachers are authorized to reproduce the practice masters in this book in limited quantity and solely for use in their own classrooms.

Printed in the USA.
Globus Printing & Packaging, Inc.
Minster, OH

Print Number: 02

Print Year: 2019